To,

Grand Master
Woo JinJung

Eastern Spirit, Western Dreams

ISBN 1-59298-090-2

Library of Congress Catalog Number: 2004115807

Printed in the United States of America

First Printing: December 2004

07 06 05 04 03   6 5 4 3 2 1

Beaver's Pond Press, Inc.

7104 Ohms Lane, Suite 216
Edina, MN 55439
(952) 829-8818
www.beaverspondpress.com

to order, visit *www.BookHouseFulfillment.com* or call 1-800-901-3480. Reseller discounts available.

Book design by Susan Larson, Larson Design, Cedar Rapids, IA

Grand Master Woo Jin Jung can be contacted at:

New Life Fitness World
3950 Wilson Ave. SW
Cedar Rapids, IA 52404 USA

E-mail: grandmaster@jungstkd.com

Eastern Spirit, Western Dreams

WOO JIN JUNG

To the memory of my parents;

To my wife and children,
Mira, Johnny, Jea, Danny, and Jinny;

To a new generation,
Mia;

And to my Tae Kwon Do family.

Table of Contents

Acknowledgments

Part 1: Korean Beginnings

Part 2: American Dream

Part 3: Survival Game in Iowa

Part 4: Tae Kwon Do

Part 5: Journeying Back

Part 6: Into the Health Club Business

Part 7: East Meets West

Epilogue   221

Acknowledgments

This book tells the story of my life, providing information on the experiences and choices that have shaped me and led me along the path I have taken. Many people have touched my heart and my life; it is an impossible task to list them all. But I want to at least acknowledge a small number of those who have helped me along the way.

A special thanks to my Tae Kwon Do family, including John Becker, Joe Houtz, Eric Heintz, Kaye Bair, Tate and Angie Klemish, Lynn Sackett, and all the other students and instructors who have come through the doors of Jung's Tae Kwon Do Academy since it opened in 1973. I treasure the classes, the tests, the tournaments, the demonstrations, and the moments and memories we have shared.

Thanks to my New Life Fitness World staff, especially Randy Snook, Mike O'Keefe, and Sandy Akers Cox, for the many hours you have devoted to the success and growth of my fitness business.

Thank you to all of New Life Fitness World's many members. Your interest in health and fitness is forever inspirational.

Many thanks to *Tae Kwon Do Times* subscribers, whose dedication to the martial arts is so important to the continuity and growth of the art of Tae Kwon Do.

Much gratitude to my business associates, with special recognition to Master Chung Kim, Dr. Yang Ahn, Mayor Donald Canney, and Steve Bright.

Thanks to Valerie Jennings Jung, Chu Woo Park, and Yen Hee Lee, for assisting me in telling my story in the first edition of this book, and to Christopher H. Jang, for translating my story.

Thank you to Mary McDonell for your preparation of this second edition for publication, and to Claudia Smith for your expertise, advice and enthusiasm, and for coordinating with the publisher.

Thank you to my family for your consistent patience and support as I followed my *Eastern Spirit, Western Dreams*.

Part 1: Korean Beginnings

Chapter 1

Soy Sauce, Tree Bark, and American Chocolate

It was 1941 and my 44-year-old mother was distressed to learn that she was pregnant with her sixth child. Most Korean women married in their late teens and finished childbearing before they reached age 30; pregnancy after age 40 was not very socially acceptable. The thought of becoming a mockery in her village was difficult for my mother to bear. She worried about causing embarrassment to her family. She also knew that having another mouth to feed would be a tremendous hardship.

The economy was in bad condition and many families were starving due to the Japanese government's control over Korea during the preceding 30 years. The Japanese confiscated over half of all Koreans' earnings during those times. Officials estimated annual production at each farm prior to harvest. Farmers were then required to provide produce based on the estimate; sometimes the estimate was much too high. There was not nearly enough left to feed the farmer and his family after the government received its allotment. It was a very bitter and humbling experience for Koreans to endure, and it would make it even more difficult for my family to afford to take care of me.

My mother considered her options. She remembered overhearing a conversation among a group of women in the village that some miscarriages were caused by consuming large quantities of soy sauce. My mother felt this was a reasonable choice because soy sauce was one item most Koreans had in abundance. But after drinking nearly a pint of the brown liquid she was unsuccessful. Ironically, I enjoy soy sauce on many of my foods today!

My mother tried a few other techniques she'd heard about that might end an unwanted pregnancy, but she was unsuccessful. Eventually my mother accepted her pregnancy.

I was born on February 20, 1942, and my mother was very loving and devoted to me for the rest of her life. I honor her for the difficulties she faced and the choices she made to serve her family's needs.

Lessons from the Country

I consider myself a farm boy. I was born and raised in a small village set in the countryside of Korea. Like so many Korean communities, our little town had a mountain, a small stream, farmland, and railroad tracks running through the village itself.

We depended on the train. It even served as a means of telling time. Unfortunately, when the train was late we were late too.

I am thankful for the time I spent growing up in the country and the lessons I learned about life and business. I quickly experienced the importance of diligence and perseverance during planting season. We all worked from dawn to dark every night in order to have plentiful crops. An old farmer in my village once told me that even the dead go to work during the sowing season. The concept of hard work stuck with me, and I have applied it to the challenges and tasks that have faced me throughout my life.

Growing up as a farm boy also taught me common sense, something that is not so common to come by. People who grow up in the city don't always get the opportunity to learn about the simpler things in life, such as nature. Farmers learn to distinguish between changing seasons and weather patterns and rely on their animal instincts to detect danger.

I applied these simple, commonsense approaches to business later on in life. When I meet people today, I like to find out where they were raised. In my opinion, there is so much more to an individual than education and work experience. I find that anyone who has had the good fortune to spend his or her childhood in a rural area tends to have strength of character and a good work ethic.

The Strength of Silence

Growing up, I rarely heard my father utter a word, and I never conversed with him for longer than ten minutes at a time. My parents were so busy working that they never took breaks for conversation, even after we hired some extra help. If I could have recorded every word my father said during the 62 years of his life it probably wouldn't have filled even one cassette tape.

My father never attended school and, like so many Koreans at that time, he could not read or write. Despite his lack of education, he did all he could to ensure that his children went to school, and he worked day and night to pay for our education.

Although my father was a typical authoritative patriarch, he had a soft spot for me, his youngest son. He often expressed his love for me through small caring gestures. We do not have any photos of him. My mother once told me that he wouldn't allow her to take any pictures of him because he said such photos would have no real value.

One of my most poignant childhood memories is of the arrest of my father during Japan's control of Korea. Two Japanese officials arrived at our farm, taking my father into custody for allegedly not providing enough produce to the government. It was shocking and painful for me to watch helplessly as this happened to my father, a man of the highest integrity.

My mother married my father when she was just 17. She was the backbone of our family and inherited the duties of a matriarch. Because my father was the oldest son in his family, my mother took on the responsibility of taking care of my grandparents, four uncles, two aunts, plus her own six children. My mother rarely slept more than four hours a night, and she labored every day of her life. She grew cotton plants, tended a small vegetable garden, and made all of our clothes herself. She was always generous to others and never sent a family guest away empty-handed. My mother seemed genuinely happy and embraced life. She was dedicated and kind to our grandparents and never raised her voice to my father, which was the norm for women during her generation. She gave up her family to take care of my father's family and her own children; she visited her own parents only once a year.

Even though my family worked hard to provide for us, we often ran short of supplies during the winter and were forced to eat tree bark and plant roots for nourishment. This was common in our village until World War II ended in 1945. Conditions improved after the war, when Korea became an independent nation. We no longer had to send the fruits of our beloved country to Japan.

Chocolate Bars and Photographs

On June 25, 1950, the Korean War broke out and Communist North Korea invaded South Korea. I was barely nine years old, but I remember it was difficult to know the details of the war because of the lack of any reliable communications system. Soon after the first flood of rumors we experienced the war firsthand: our home was converted into a campsite for refugees.

My family decided not to evacuate the village even after the battles moved as close as 40 miles north of our home. The school I attended was transformed into a M.A.S.H. facility. Our classes were then held by the local stream or even in the cemetery. After school my friends and I spent our leisure time counting the number of planes flying overhead. Some days more than 100 airplanes clouded the sky above our community.

North Korea appeared to be winning the war before the United States joined the United Nations forces. It was the first time many Koreans had encountered Americans, and vice versa. I remember staring at the soldiers with much curiosity. They watched us in return. I recall one occasion when an American soldier watched in apparent disbelief as a Korean woman carried her luggage on top of her head. I guess the differences were strange for both cultures.

It wasn't long before I overcame my fears of the American soldiers. I followed them around, hoping I would be given chocolate candy or even cigarettes. I learned a little English and would shout at them, "Chocolate give me!" or "Cigarette give me!" I still recall how good those chocolate bars tasted.

I enjoyed all the luxuries the Americans brought with them, especially the ham and sweet jam. I once sliced my tongue when attempting to lick some remnants of jam from a container that was thrown from a passing military train. There was one curious black powder that I didn't like, and rightly so; I learned that it wasn't supposed to be eaten, but should have been brewed into coffee.

I saw a camera for the first time in my life when a U.S. soldier took pictures of some nearby children swarming for food. I learned a lot about Americans during those hot summer days, but the one thing I couldn't quite get over were the soldiers' hairy backs and chests. It also horrified most Korean women to see these men without their shirts on.

Americans were unfamiliar to me, but I learned to appreciate their efforts to save South Korea. My memories of the war include my overwhelming feeling of gratitude toward the soldiers and the country that sent them. Some 33,700 American soldiers died in the Korean War, fighting far from home for a land that did not belong to them. This made an impression on me, and I have never forgotten the sacrifices made by the United States and the military personnel who served in Korea. I have wanted to contribute in some measure to repaying the debt of gratitude I feel is owed by Koreans to Americans.

The Price of Hunger

The casualties of war affected most Korean families, including ours. One day during the peak of the war my mother cooked a beef dish with rice. I knew something special was happening because she only made this particular dinner once a year; this time she prepared enough for only one person. It was served to my second oldest brother. He had been drafted for the Korean Army and my mother wanted to fix him one last meal before he left. I sat next to him and watched while he devoured the beef dish; I hoped he might leave some scraps for me.

My thoughts were far from the reality of the moment. All I could think about was having some of the delicious red meat on his plate. The opportunity to have such good food was rare during the war.

My brother did not finish his meal. He thoughtfully left me alone to consume the rest of his dinner. I was so busy eating that I missed his departure and never had the opportunity to say good-bye. I still am sorry for my selfish behavior; I regret not having been there to wish him well before he left.

Every day while my brother was gone my parents worried. When we received a letter from him the family would gather together to listen to my oldest brother read the news. The letters were all written by friends of his in the Army since he, like my father, could not read or write. In 1953, the last letter arrived. We had not heard from him in quite a while and had wondered whether he was alive or dead.

It was soon after the arrival of his last letter that we received a letter from the government notifying us of my brother's death. My oldest brother was devastated to have to be the one to share the horrible news with my parents. He waited a long time before telling anyone in the family about it. My mother took it exceptionally hard and refused to accept her son's death for 20 years after the war. She hung on, hoping that my brother had been captured by the North Koreans and was alive somewhere in a prison camp. My dad's health quickly deteriorated and he passed away after my brother died.

I learned a valuable lesson from my brother's passing. I discovered that losing loved ones leaves a void so deep in our hearts that even fame and fortune cannot fill that place.

Chapter 2

School Days and Farmer Ways

In the winter of 1958, I left my childhood village behind and began an unexpected journey to a new city. My family could not afford for me to continue my education after middle school since my two oldest brothers were already attending high school in Busan, a nearby city.

It was difficult for my mother to ask of me, but I knew I had to quit school. One day she sat all of us down and said, "We cannot send three of you to school, but I don't know what to do." After a long, uncomfortable pause, I said, "I am still young and will probably have another chance to go to school, so I will stay at home and help." With that said I became a farmer. While most of my friends went off to receive a formal education, wearing their school uniforms, I wore scruffy work clothes and went to the field to labor on our farm.

I hated farming and I detested it even more when I saw my old school friends. I even tried to avoid them. I couldn't wait for the day when I didn't have to be a farmer any more, but I wasn't sure what else I would do. I knew one thing: farmers in Korea were always poor and I wasn't going to live penniless.

The Runaway Farm Boy

After a miserable year of farming it was time for me to take the high school entrance exam. It was a difficult test to pass even for the most intelligent students. Although I desperately wanted to go back to high school, I was extremely concerned that I would not pass the exam. I decided I would just have to find time to study, and yet that was not what concerned me the most. It was my family's expectation that I would go to an agricultural school that was more frustrating for me. They knew that college was out of the question and thought farming was a skill that I should perfect.

I was a hopeless case for the next several days. I spent hours crying at my father's grave and sometimes refused to leave my bed, hoping that I would find an answer to change my mother's expectations.

Eventually, I had to pick up a load of fertilizer from the agricultural warehouse. I loaded the fertilizer onto a *jaegae*, which was a wooden A-frame device used for hauling. It was a dreadful job, carrying a heavy load of rank fertilizer on my back for 12 miles. I thought to myself, I will die before I do this again. Then, something drastic came over me and I smashed the *jaegae* to pieces. I knew immediately that my mother and oldest brother would scold me for breaking the farm equipment and for being an irresponsible farmer. I started to run. I ran and ran until I heard the train whistle blow.

Without thinking twice, I snuck onto the train and risked getting caught without a ticket. I did not care. It was better than being punished at home, and I watched without regret as my farmer days disappeared into the distance.

Chapter 3

From Bullied to Black Belt to Bully

The train pulled into South Korea's second largest city, Busan, a harbor community located at the southern tip of the country. I cautiously departed the train and slipped out of the station toward my sister's house in Suhmyun, a nearby neighborhood.

My 33-year-old widowed sister lived alone. She never remarried after her husband died, mainly because remarriage was considered taboo in Korea. She ran a small bakery and sold traditional Korean cakes called *yugwa*. When I arrived she seemed very confused to see me, but nonetheless she gave me a warm welcome.

Like a starved wolf I inhaled the food she prepared, eating until my stomach was full. She listened calmly by my side as I explained to her how I ended up in Busan. "You went through a lot," she said. "It is a little crowded here, but if it is fine with you, you are welcome to stay with me."

My sister also helped me study for the high school entrance exam, and I soon found it was even more difficult to prepare for than I originally imagined. It was no surprise when I heard that I failed the admission test for Busan Industrial High School, one of the top institutions in the city, but I did pass a second round of exams and was accepted into Kyung Nam Industrial High School. I enjoyed fixing machinery and knew that attending the industrial school would further develop my skills.

Kyung Nam High was not exactly what I had hoped for. I soon became a center of ridicule and was beaten up on a regular basis by the school bullies. My strong accent revealed my country roots, and the students called me a yokel. I was in so many fights that my bruised body never had a chance to recover from the black-and-blue markings before the next beating occurred. I became so insecure during class that I spoke as little as possible so the bullies wouldn't poke fun at me. Besides being a farm boy, I was also short and skinny, making me an easy target to pick on. The few times I did stand my ground with the scrappers actually made things worse. After school the entire gang would wait to seek their revenge on me. During those days, bullies were everywhere in Korea and many innocent students felt the wrath of their abuse.

I was too embarrassed to tell my sister about the beatings and I feared if I told her she would pull me out of class. So I searched for a solution on my own. My persistence to resolve this problem grew when I learned that a close friend of mine missed a day of school to nurse his wounds from the night before. I was furious: my blood began to boil and my heart pounded. I had to put a stop to these menaces. I spent several days considering ways to get even with the bullies. I finally decided to learn martial arts.

Tae Kwon Do is a traditional Korean martial art that only a handful of people knew at the time. I saved my money until I finally had enough to enroll at one of the local martial arts schools. It would be a dream come true when I could finally defend myself against the bullies, and I believed that Tae Kwon Do would make that dream a reality. Unfortunately, the students taking martial arts were the hoodlums and gangsters from my neighborhood and I was required to respect them. Tae Kwon Do is based on seniority; newer students are expected to be subservient to their more experienced peers. If they did not follow this rule, then it was grounds for punishment.

Since I was a beginner, the senior students seemed to treat me like I had some kind of disease. I was forced to do all sorts of errands for them, like mopping the floor, cleaning the gym, getting drinks, picking up snacks, and fetching buckets of water so they could wash their feet. It was a very humiliating experience and it was all I could do to go to class, but the thought of defending myself kept me focused.

I learned basic martial arts techniques and forms, and how to be a human sandbag. The seniors often made me stand in front of them so they could use my body to sharpen their punching and kicking skills, frequently knocking me to the ground. During the Korean War, Tae Kwon Do became very popular, especially for Koreans living in Busan, where life was extremely dangerous. Knowing martial arts was one way people could protect themselves and stay alive. However, not everyone is cut out for Tae Kwon Do. It takes a lot of will, stamina, and dedication. I learned to persevere despite these obstacles, and I was eventually considered an equal among my peers.

Black Belt

In spring 1959, I earned my black belt, 14 months after my first martial arts class. My peers rewarded me with a party at one of the local restaurants. To this day I still remember how good the food tasted.

Now that I was officially a black belt I felt confident that I could defend myself. I went from a fearful skinny kid to an arrogant showoff. I felt in charge. I carried my Tae Kwon Do uniform on my back and proudly displayed my black belt in front of the bullies. No one messed with me or made fun of my strange accent. I often greeted people with a cold stare, and they kept their distance from me.

Becoming a Bully

My attitude changed for the worse after I received my black belt. I became one of the school tyrants and chummed around with the other neighborhood scrappers. We even started charging people money to protect them from the other gangs in the city. It was a good source of income at the time, especially in a place as dangerous as Busan.

I hung out in the alleys with one group of gangsters who smoked cigarettes, got into fights, and engaged in some illegal activities. After nearly six months of this and spending the night in jail several times, I decided it was time for a change. I knew that no matter how much I pretended to be a bully, I was still that soft-hearted yokel from the country. After I announced to the group that I was leaving, I faced a series of threats for almost a year, but nothing materialized and I never went back to being a bully.

I learned a lot of valuable lessons during those six months of being a bully. I felt shameful and dishonorable for lying to my sister about my grades, abusing my body and soul, and being a hoodlum. But I did learn an important truth: Tae Kwon Do should never be used against innocent people; it should be used to help them against the dishonest and violent. I pledged to myself that I would uphold this truth until death.

Chapter 4

Rice Cakes and Bean Sprouts

High school graduation was approaching and I still didn't know what I was going to do with my future. I had three options: return to the village where I grew up and become a farmer, attend a college that I could not afford, or find a job at a machine shop.

Finding a good job was next to impossible in Korea at the time. Most of the industrial buildings had been destroyed during the war and the economy was extremely bad for recent graduates. Despite these obstacles, I felt getting a job was the only realistic option.

At one point I considered working in a factory. A few of my school friends had jobs there, but they were working like dogs and still had barely enough money to make ends meet. This did not seem much better than being a farmer.

My whole life became a blur as I fretted about which path to take. The only thing that eased my mind was punching the sandbags at the martial arts school. After some time I just could not bear to think about my future any more.

Then, in winter 1961, I was forced to sell rice cakes on the street corner for money. Graduation was only a few months away and my oldest brother was having a difficult time paying for the remainder of my tuition, so I decided to help out. I felt terrible burdening him, especially when I knew he was struggling. Most of the other kids were earning money selling newspapers, but I wanted to sell something that didn't compete with their sales.

After much discussion with my friends we decided to do what no other kid would do: sell rice cakes. It was extremely embarrassing to shout "rice cakes" from the street, but we had to do it anyway. I actually liked the idea of this challenge and thought it might shed some light on my future.

But when I walked through the neighborhood I could not bring myself to yell "rice cakes." My voice became softer than a spring breeze. I just could not do it. My friends experienced the same problem and none of us made any sales that night. Instead we ate all of the cakes that we were supposed to sell for profit.

On the second night we had the same issues, but by the third evening things were different: we were desperate and could not afford to eat our profits. We had to make some sales. I took a deep breath and shouted, "rice cakes." I was surprised to hear my own voice. I finally had found the courage to sell the rice cakes.

Now, with confidence on my side, I slowly began selling the cakes in the local neighborhood and soon I extended my sales to customers miles away. I encountered all kinds of people during those nights: happy, sad, healthy, sick, poor, wealthy. I met poor people who seemed wealthy, and rich people who appeared to be poor. I soon wondered what kind of person I would become in life.

After selling rice cakes for several weeks, I still did not know what type of profession to take up. I then realized if I wanted to be a big fish in a big pond, I had to swim in the largest pool of water. I had to go to the biggest city in Korea: my destination had to be Seoul.

My Oldest Brother's Priceless Gift

I left Busan for Seoul on February 26, 1962, twenty days after graduating from high school. I did not work during those days; I stayed home instead. It turned out to be the last 20-day vacation of my life.

While my oldest brother and I waited for my train to arrive, he handed me an envelope full of cash. I knew from the size of it that there was a large amount enclosed. I opened the envelope, took out about half of the money, and gave the envelope back to him. I knew he could not afford such a large amount. He refused to take it and insisted that I keep it. I later found out that my brother risked his job and reputation as a train station ticket attendant to give me a day's worth of ticket sales without permission. He had a great deal of difficulty borrowing money to pay back the station for what he had taken.

The night train arrived in Seoul early the next morning. When I exited the train, I stood mesmerized in the middle of the city's large train station. Some beggars slept near the wall, and the air was cold and damp. I stayed at a relative's house that night and got up the next morning to go exploring. I was surprised to see how busy the streets were and how differently people dressed and looked compared to the people in Busan.

I was desperate to find a job right away, and decided to apply the same logic I used when I sold rice cakes. I needed to figure out what I could sell that nobody else really wanted to sell. While I was pondering the idea I heard someone shout, "bean sprouts!"

"That's it! I will sell bean sprouts." The demand for bean sprouts had increased since the war because they were so inexpensive. I wanted to get started right away. The next morning I went to see a local bean-sprout wholesaler in the city. He reluctantly agreed to give me three buckets to sell, instead of the usual four.

"Experienced people sell four buckets a day," he said. "But since you are new at this you should take only three."

I asked him how much four buckets would cost. I then told

him, "No, give me four."

He replied, "You probably can't even sell three. You should just take three and not waste your money."

I was not ready to give up. "I can sell four if others can sell four," I argued. "Please give me four buckets."

He stared at me for a moment and finally decided I could have four. The wholesaler also told me about a hilly route that the other sellers refused to take. He said I should try that area first to see how I would do.

An unwelcome bitter wind struck me as I stepped outside the warehouse and started on my journey. The weather was brutally cold; it was so frigid my pants froze from the water dripping off the buckets. I felt like I might just break down, but I knew I couldn't give up.

I tried to shout, "bean sprouts," but my voice failed. It was just like when I started selling rice cakes. I tried again, but there was nothing. My body felt weak and heavy. It was all I could do to carry the buckets of sprouts. I trudged along, my legs wobbly, up and down the hilly streets all morning without making a sale. I tried to pry my frozen lips apart to yell bean sprouts again, when I tasted something salty in my mouth. I was crying. Tears were running down my cheeks. It was the first time I had cried since I left home three years earlier.

Just when I was feeling at my lowest I heard someone call for me, "Hey, bean-sprout seller!" I was so shocked I couldn't move. "Are you going to sell the sprouts or not?" she asked. "Yes," I thought, and I ran over to her to make my first sale. I felt revived, and began shouting "bean sprouts" at the top of my lungs, attracting more and more customers.

One day while I was on my way to make a few sales, I was confronted by a girl in the alleyway. The alley was extremely narrow and could only accommodate one of us to pass through at a time.

The girl stared at me and I stared back. We looked about the same age. After exchanging stares she said, "I am late for work. Are you going to move or just stand there?"

In Korea, it was customary to move out of the way for people with disabilities or those carrying heavy loads, but she did not fit either of these categories. I retaliated and said, "Can't you see these buckets? You should move and let me go first." I made a sudden movement forward and she backed away. As I passed by her she grumbled that I ruined her skirt.

I started to feel badly about yelling at the girl, but I brushed it off by rationalizing that we were both having a bad day. In retrospect, I think I would have reacted differently if I had grown up in America, where chivalry is a part of life. I realize that chivalrous behavior is just not a high priority in eastern cultures.

I soon had regular customers waiting for me on the corner each morning. At night, I slept for free in a room attached to the bean warehouse. It was a tiny, crowded space housing several other sellers, but it was perfect for me. The other occupants were not pleased to add me to the small space and even started displaying hostility. I relied on what had worked for me in the past: I informed them that I was a black belt in Tae Kwon Do and they should not mess with me. None of them caused me any more trouble.

Chapter 5

Juggling Jobs

I sold bean sprouts for 15 days. One of my most dedicated customers was a housemaid who had an accent very similar to mine. I asked her one day, "Are you from Kyung Sang province?"

"Yes, I am," she said with a smile. "And the owner of this house is from there as well."

She seemed glad to have met me and I was happy to have made her acquaintance too. I felt close to her, knowing that we came from similar worlds.

The following morning I saw her again. While we were reminiscing about our hometowns I heard a grinding noise from the house. The sound was familiar to me and I asked the housemaid where the noise was coming from. She explained that the owner of the house operated a small iron foundry inside.

I quickly finished the rest of my morning route and went straight to the public bathhouse to clean up. It was the first bath I had taken since arriving in Seoul. I put on the best clothes I owned and went back to the iron foundry. The maid didn't recognize me when she first opened the door. She had only seen me wearing my work clothes, with a towel wrapped around my forehead.

When she finally made the connection she smiled and asked, "Aren't you the bean-sprout man?"

"Yes," I replied. "Can I possibly see the owner? Please don't tell him I sell bean sprouts; just tell him that someone wants to meet him." She paused for a moment, went inside, and quickly came back to take me to him. The iron foundry was bigger than I expected. The owner, a mild-mannered man, was sitting in the middle of a garden.

I knelt down in front of him and said, "I graduated from an industrial high school near Busan and I came to Seoul to make something of myself. If you give me a chance to work at your foundry, I will work hard," I pleaded. "If you provide me with food and a place to sleep you do not even have to pay me until you feel I am worthy."

The owner looked at me with a puzzled face and replied, "I admire your ambition, young man!" I was told to start the next day, and he made arrangements for me to live in a small room next to the shop. I later learned that a younger man sitting next to the iron owner was his lazy brother-in-law, who had not attempted to find a job after graduation. The owner used me as an example to show his brother-in-law that many people in Korea were desperate to be working.

The fact that I was not getting paid was not a problem for me. I believed that this job would provide me with the experience necessary to get a good-paying position the next time. I soon discovered that ironwork was much more difficult than I had thought, and my co-workers were trying their hardest to make my life miserable.

The most difficult part of the job was that I didn't know the slang terms for the shop tools. Instead, I referred to them by their proper names, as I had learned in school. This really irritated the ironworkers. They often asked me to grab tools for them, and I never knew which ones to get. They tormented me for my mistakes by hitting me over the head with tools until blood rolled down my face. I realized they were going to make this experience a living hell for as long as I continued to work at the foundry.

My responsibilities included running all the errands, cleaning the shop, and putting the equipment away at the end of the day. There was never any hot water left for me to scrub my black, greasy hands. Despite the humiliation, I was given an opportunity to work on the lathe machine after just two months. Most of my co-workers had worked there longer and still weren't allowed to touch the machine for their first six months. Ironically, after my assignment to the lathe machine, my counterparts stopped abusing me.

Going to College

Although I actually came to enjoy working at the iron foundry, I had another dream. I wanted to go to college.

After working at the shop for three months I found a better job at a larger factory. It turned out that a distant relative of mine was managing a plant, and he decided to give me a position there. The foundry owner, his wife, and the maid were all sorry to see me go, and even though I was not a paid employee, the owner's wife gave me some money before I left. The first item I bought with the cash was a small alarm clock. I couldn't afford to be late for my new job at Wooil Chemical Inc.

The company of 300 employees manufactured plastic household products. OK Toothpaste and OK Toothbrushes, very popular brands in Korea, were the factory's top sellers. Even though the plant was much larger than the foundry, the working conditions were about the same. Without labor unions, there were no safety regulations.

There were two shifts, each 12 hours a day. Every employee was expected to work the morning shift one week and the night shift the next. Approximately 80 percent of the workers were young girls who came to Seoul to help support their families. A lot of them struggled with the heavy workload and the rotating schedule. They would collapse in the small room they shared with five or six other girls at the end of their shifts. They sent all of their money to their families, except for a small amount that they saved to cover their room and board. I thought of my own sister and felt sorry for these young working girls. Several months later a series of labor disputes erupted across the country and I risked my job to stand with the unions.

During all the chaos, I began thinking about the impossible. There were still 12 hours left in the day after my work shift. I was not used to having extra time and I wanted to allocate my additional hours for college.

I started scouting out junior colleges in the area and came across a newspaper advertisement for a technical school. One evening after working the night shift, I bought a box of OK Toothpaste and went to the admissions office at the Sudo Technical College. I placed the toothpaste in front of the attendant and said, "I work at a factory that makes this toothpaste. Help me get into college. I work twelve hours a day and don't know if I can afford school, but I would really like to study." I walked out, leaving him sitting there with the toothpaste and with a look of shock on his face.

I knew one thing for certain: even if I didn't get into that school, he would think about me every morning when he brushed his teeth. Finally, after much anticipation, I was accepted into the technical college. I am still not sure if it was because I passed the entrance exam or if it was the toothpaste. I didn't care; I was a college student. My mother was elated to hear the news, but she was also concerned for my well-being. She thought I was working too much and that adding classes would push me even more and might even endanger my health.

Courtesy and the Three Jobs

Now that I was in school I had to find a second source of

income to pay for tuition. I found a job tutoring my relative's four children, but I was more in the position of being a moral guide to them than being an academic teacher.

The kids ranged in age from preschool to fourth grade. I woke them early in the morning for chores, and I taught them discipline, manners, respect for elders, and other Confucian teachings. To their parents' satisfaction, the children soon became very well-behaved.

Six months passed and I decided to make another leap of faith. If attending a junior college was as difficult as obtaining a degree from a four-year school then I didn't want to settle for less than a four-year degree. So I transferred to Hanyang University's Engineering School and enrolled in night classes.

To put it mildly, I had no life. I put in 12 hours at the plant and then dragged myself to night classes for the remainder of the day. Managing my money and sleeping became a huge struggle. When I was hungry I drank water to fill my stomach, and I slept only when I could not do anything else. I took naps standing up on crowded buses during my commutes to school and work, and I pinched myself during class lectures to stay awake.

Bus Money and Old Friends

I could not make ends meet even with three jobs. There were days when I could not go to class because I did not have enough money for bus fare. My co-workers would ask me, "Hey, college student, aren't you going to school today?"

I was too ashamed to tell them the truth, so I would lie and say, "No, I don't have class tonight."

One particular evening I didn't have bus money so I decided to work late instead. A supervisor walked over and confronted me about not going to school. "Did you run out of bus fare again?" He pulled a crumpled-up bill from his pocket and handed it to me.

"You better get to class right now," he said. "No excuses." I couldn't refuse; I took the money, bowed once, and hurried off.

It turned out the supervisor gave me enough cash to pay for 10 bus rides every month. Thanks to his kind heart I never had to miss class again. There were others who also helped me out during those tough times. During a monthly walk-through, the president of the factory stopped by to observe my milling work. He turned to the supervisor and asked, "Did we have a machine that automatically greased oil during the milling process before?"

"No," the supervisor replied. "Woo Jin made this device himself."

The president stepped closer to me and asked, "You made this yourself?"

"Yes, sir," I said.

"How did you make it?"

"I saw another model at night school that had a self-greasing component. Since this machine was missing that piece, I found some old equipment in the back room and attached the parts to it."

"Well done," he said with a nod.

It was soon after our encounter that I couldn't make my tuition payments. I just couldn't save enough money, even though I had not wasted a penny. I anguished over my dilemma for several days and finally decided to approach the factory president about a loan.

"Mr. President," I said, "I cannot afford to pay for my education this semester and wanted to ask you if you could loan me some money. I will repay you as soon as I can."

He paused for a moment and said he would make a decision when he returned from a 10-day business trip. I was not optimistic that he would agree. After all, it was a large sum of money and there was no guarantee that I would be able to repay him.

Tuition was due the same day the president was scheduled to return. By then I had given up my dream of earning a college degree from the engineering school. But the morning after he returned I was called into his office. The president handed me an envelope without saying a word. I was elated. It was enough money for me to finish my degree.

Thirty years later, I found the plant supervisor in the United States and asked him, "How do I repay you for the bus money you loaned me?"

He said, "You already have. All I wanted was to see you well and successful."

I located the company president many years after that. He had sold the factory and was living in the local area. He didn't remember helping me 39 years earlier, but I reminded him that I would not have graduated from college if it weren't for his kindness. He said to me, "You don't have to repay me, but instead help others like yourself."

I cried like a small child as I remembered how desperate I once was. I did as the plant president requested: I established the Woo Jin Jung Scholarship Fund for students who cannot afford college and for families of cancer patients. I would not be where I am today if it had not been for those who helped me along the way. That is a kindness I want to pass along.

Tae Kwon Do in the Factory Yard

Time was the most precious commodity in my life. Time spent sleeping and meeting other needs I kept to a bare minimum. It was all I could do to keep up with work and school, but I still had one more desire to fulfill: renewing my devotion to Tae Kwon Do.

For the first time since I moved to Seoul, I put on my Tae Kwon Do uniform and began practicing martial arts every day in the factory yard. I could feel my energy level rising with each kick, punch, and yell. The factory yard became my own paradise where I could feel confident and at peace again.

One afternoon, a small group of workers approached while I was practicing and asked if I could teach them martial arts. They said they had wanted to learn for some time, but could not afford to take lessons. I didn't have the heart to turn them away and wanted to share with them the wonderful joys of Tae Kwon Do. My co-workers insisted that they pay me a small amount of money for their lessons. After they showed much persistence, I agreed. I accepted a third of what most gyms charged for such classes.

More plant employees joined my martial arts classes. Later on, even the local residents started participating. Soon the Tae Kwon Do classes grew to a dozen students. Most of the students practiced in street clothes and work boots or sandals, making it difficult for them to kick properly. Some nights I had to cancel class due to rain, or even because there was not enough moonlight to adequately light the practice area. It was a pretty pathetic sight, but we managed to get by somehow.

Tae Kwon Do School in Jail

The warden at the local jail requested to see me one day. When I started to introduce myself he interrupted to request information about my martial arts classes. "I saw you instructing students the other night at the factory."

I worried about the unreported fees I had collected from classes. "I am happy to see people learning Tae Kwon Do," the warden said. "It must be difficult to teach lessons in the dark. You know, there is an old bomb shelter in the jail, built by the Japanese Army when they occupied Korea," he said. "You are welcome to use it if you like. We have no use for it anymore. This neighborhood is full of crime and it wouldn't hurt a few more people to learn martial arts."

Although I was extremely thankful for his offer, I was terribly disappointed when I saw the awful condition of the shelter. I decided to accept his offer anyway, and I thanked him for his generosity.

The warden provided 15 prisoners to help rebuild the bomb shelter. The inmates worked hard during the first few days and made a lot of progress, but after that they didn't accomplish anything. I asked one of the prisoners why they had stopped working. He said it was because I wasn't providing them with cigarettes. I knew smoking in the jail or giving them cigarettes was against the rules, but if I wanted my gym finished I had to play their game.

I brought the inmates two packs of cigarettes every morning. They divided them up equally among themselves before smoking them. Luckily for me, the prisoners preferred the cheap brand, because cheap cigarettes were usually stronger compared to the more expensive kinds. When they were short on matches, they used small stones and cotton to light the cigarettes. I am sure the guards knew what I was doing, but they never said a word.

It took three months of hard work and over 100 packs of cigarettes before my first Tae Kwon Do gym was complete. We built a new floor, painted the walls, installed a few fluorescent lights, and even cleaned up a few actual skeletons and other remains from the war.

From that day forward, the old bomb shelter became a haven for students practicing martial arts every night. The three other Tae Kwon Do schools in the neighborhood started losing members to my do jang since I didn't charge people to join. I taught every class during college breaks and let an assistant master teach while I was in school.

Later on, the warden approached me about teaching martial arts to some teenagers who had been in trouble with the law. I couldn't refuse. After all, it was his generosity that made the Tae Kwon Do school possible. The kids were a lot to manage at first, but as I saw them develop into productive members of society it all became worthwhile.

Part 2: American Dream

Chapter 6

Soldier in a Divided Nation

In the spring of 1966, I received a letter from the Korean Army notifying me that I must return home for a physical exam and prepare for service in the armed forces. I would have to put my third year of college on hold and face my family for the first time in years. I wanted them to think I had made it big and decided to make a grand entrance by flying into Busan instead of taking a train or bus.

I was just a 25-year-old fool, full of hot air and looking to feel important. I wanted everyone to believe that I was successful, not just a factory worker and Tae Kwon Do instructor. So, for the first time in my life, I took a propeller airplane to the Busan airport, where my childhood friends and family were waiting for me. It pleased me to see my peers looking so envious of me and also to see my mother's proud face as I stepped off that plane. For a moment it seemed worth having to pay off the cost of the airplane ticket for the next several months.

Rat Tails and Basic Training

At the first day of basic training, the staff sergeant asked if anyone knew Tae Kwon Do. I was so excited to hear the question that I raised my hand before he could finish. He doubtfully asked to see my black belt certificate and I happily presented my fourth-degree belt certification to him. "Is this real?" the sergeant asked.

"Yes, sir!" I yelled back. "Should I demonstrate a kick for you?"

"Fine, you are now a platoon leader," he said.

And just like that I became a team leader of 50 new recruits. I was ordered to attend my first meeting that afternoon. When I arrived, the sergeant announced that each platoon was to collect five tails from rats by the next morning. It was a very peculiar request, but no one dared to question it and we left to organize our groups for the rat search. There were no rats to be found. We searched and searched and didn't come up with one tail. I dreamt that night about battling hundreds of the rodents. By early morning I started preparing my team for the punishment we were sure to receive for not completing the mission.

Surprisingly, a few of the platoon leaders held up five rats' tails and were dismissed, but the rest of us were severely beaten. After the meeting I went to see one of my peers to find out how he had located the tails. It was simple: he bought them from the sergeant. The Korean Army was completely corrupt. After learning the truth, I met with my trainees and discussed creating an emergency money fund to prevent future beatings. I regularly gave a portion of our collections to the staff sergeant, which I'm sure he gave to other officers.

Toward the end of the basic training program we were informed that the platoon leaders would be fulfilling new responsibilities for the remainder of the session. I was hoping to be reassigned to a technical project so I could use my skills. The process was corrupt and I would have to buy my way into a new position, so I went to a military snack shop, bought one of the cheapest items, and asked for small bills. I put the money in an envelope and left to meet with the assignment officer.

As we were discussing some favorable possibilities for me, I slipped the bulging envelope into the officer's pocket. He seemed very satisfied with the package of money and took me to the office for an assignment. I was sent to maintain the military vehicles at the Fleet Management Division, near Busan.

I still smile today when I imagine the assignment officer's expression when he opened the fat envelope that actually contained very little money. I certainly would have loved to have seen it, but luckily for me I was already on my way to Busan.

I am not proud of what I did, though. In a way I believe my actions were no different from those of the staff sergeant. Fortunately, I do not believe there is so much corruption in the Korean Army today.

Tae Kwon Do for All Soldiers

I was hoping when I reported for duty at the Fleet Management Division that I would have an opportunity to work on military vehicles, but that wasn't the case. After about four weeks in Busan, the commanding general notified me that I would be teaching Tae Kwon Do to other soldiers.

About a year before I joined the Army, General Choi Hong Hi implemented a policy that all Korean soldiers must learn martial arts. I was soon teaching my fellow soldiers as well as army officers the skills of Tae Kwon Do, and I discovered that I had much more authority over the armed forces than some of my superiors. Unfortunately, my cushy position did not last long. After about a year, our unit was transferred to the Demilitarized Zone (DMZ) at the 38th parallel, replacing another unit that was reassigned to Vietnam.

Life was not as easy there, but I did learn to appreciate the beautiful sites of my country during my days off. It is still difficult for me to accept Korea's division. While I was carrying out my guard duties there I pledged that I would someday work to reunite my country.

Transfer to Vietnam

Soon after I moved to the DMZ, I heard rumors that Korea was sending troops to Vietnam. Originally, the Army had only sent medical units and other auxiliary forces, but now it was sending troops to help fight the war against the Viet Cong. I was becoming more and more eager to go, so I decided to enlist as a volunteer martial arts instructor. Even to be allowed to participate as a volunteer I had to go through a rigorous screening process that included fighting another black belt. Just before we were to start sparring I said to my opponent, "As long as we both show a good effort we will pass the test. Let's take it easy."

The soldier said it sounded like a good idea since he had not practiced in awhile. But as soon as the bell rang, he charged at me like a raging bull. I was unexpectedly taken off guard and got beaten up pretty badly. Fortunately, we both passed the test. When I returned to base I found out that only career soldiers would be eligible to teach martial arts. I was disappointed, but I enlisted to go to Vietnam anyway.

Small village where I was born. As a young boy I tended cattle, taking them to graze each day. This gave me time to think and dream about my future.

First picture ever taken, in elementary school. My family did not have a camera.

At age 16 in my high school uniform. I was a farm boy who had just arrived in the city. I found city life exciting, and I happily wore the uniform of my new school.

With a jaegae, which farmers used in place of a tractor or any modern equipment. At age fifteen, I became frustrated while working in the field and broke the jaegae in anger. I knew I'd be in trouble, and I ran away.

Outside the Tae Kwon Do school where I first trained, the first picture taken of me in my dobok (uniform). I learned at this rustic facility that the human spirit was what mattered; comfort in training was not important. At this school the direction of my life changed and my dreams were awakened.

With the bicycle which served as my only means
of transportation to multiple jobs and school.

On the telephone
at my tire repair
shop. I am smiling,
but I remember
those days as the
most difficult of
my life, working
three jobs and
going to school.

At right in the photo, with friends who banded together after the Korean War. Such groups formed for individual and neighborhood protection. My group often provided assistance to people in need.

With a group of South Vietnamese people. These people were poor, and their homeland was ravaged by war. I would like to go back to Vietnam someday, to find out if these villagers survived the war and to meet them again.

On a helicopter in
South Vietnam in 1968.
During the Vietnam War,
I saw battle with all its
life-and-death consequences. I
am still physically
shaken at the sound of a
helicopter overhead.

Standing near a row of helicopters used in battle in Vietnam.

In Vietnam at the height of the war in 1967. Being a soldier at war required alertness 24 hours a day, every day of the week, in order to survive.

A group of us gathered to honor the memory of a soldier friend who had just been killed in Vietnam. We drank warm beer and reminisced about him. A sip of warm beer always brings back memories of Vietnam and the chaos of the war.

At the M.A.S.H. unit in Vietnam, where I spent several weeks recovering after being shot in my left leg.

With my Vietnam 'roommate.' As soldiers in Vietnam we shared a foxhole and became good friends. I lost track of this man after the war, and I continue to search for him.

My 102-year-old mother waiting for a visitor outside the family home.
When expecting a visitor, she waited patiently outside, wrapping herself in
a blanket if the weather was cold.

At one time my family home in South Korea was occupied by four generations.
My mother is in the center of the photo.

Chapter 7

America, Korea, and Vietnam

In July 1967, I boarded a U.S. Navy vessel headed for Vietnam along with 3,000 other soldiers. We crowded the ship's 200-foot-tall deck and yelled good-bye to our families. There were so many people it was impossible for me to locate my family. I scrambled to write my name on a large piece of cardboard and held it high in the air, hoping to catch my mother's eye. We simultaneously spotted each other and waved as long as our eyes could see. I learned later that my mother stood at the harbor until the ship was out of sight and cried for hours and hours after I left.

We sat in fearful silence once the vessel was out to sea, and I wondered what would become of us after we arrived in Vietnam.

Watermelon Thief

We spent 12 dreadful days and nights aboard the vessel, seven days longer than expected due to horrible weather conditions. A rumor began circulating around the ship that the Korean Marines were killing Korean Army soldiers and tossing their bodies overboard. Although there were only 200 Marines on deck, they had a treacherous reputation that kept most of us out of their sight. Eventually the gossip got so out of hand that the officers organized a Tae Kwon Do demonstration to boost morale. After that, we did not lose a single soldier.

Soon another problem surfaced. After 10 days of eating greasy, American food for the first time, we started getting sick. The 30 toilets on deck were almost always occupied. Without a partition to divide the stalls there was the constant view of sick soldiers bobbing in unison with each sway of the ship.

We all longed for some Korean food. One thing we could keep down was watermelon. The problem was that only a small piece was allocated for each of us at each meal. We wanted more, and I was determined to find it. I learned from a kitchen employee where the fruit was kept and that it was well guarded. So, that night, several of us risked going to jail to raid the stash of watermelons.

Slowly, three of us crawled toward the storage shelter. I snuck into the room where the guard was sleeping and put a knife against his throat. "Stand up, go," I said for the first time in English. The guard, standing in his underwear, followed my order without much resistance. Once we approached the storage door I told him, "Open key! Open door!"

He didn't understand. "Open door. Open door," I screamed, pointing at the lock. He finally figured it out and opened the closet.

We couldn't believe our eyes. There were more than 100 watermelons lying there, waiting to be eaten. We wanted to take them all, but our greedy hands could only carry three at a time.

As we struggled to get the precious fruits back to our quarters we realized we had left the guard unattended. If he reported us we would surely face a court martial, but fortunately he didn't. Instead he stood by the door smiling at us, letting us take as many watermelons as our hearts desired. That night, we celebrated our victory by devouring as many watermelons as our stomachs would allow.

Tae Kwon Do Instructor in Vietnam

We were all exhausted when the ship finally pulled into Da Nang, Vietnam. I tried to stay alert to my surroundings and especially to the Marines boarding the ship that we were departing. They were on their way home after serving a year in Vietnam. I noticed their eyes were bloodshot and empty, and they were wearing necklaces with shrunken ears and noses from their enemies. It became obvious to me why the North Vietnamese feared the Marines so much. They said nothing to us as they passed by, and I realized then how close to death we all might be.

Before I knew it, I was on Vietnamese soil. I took a deep breath and said to myself, I have to be alert to stay alive. I must leave here alive. I stepped forward with my left foot, the same way every military march begins. I knew that when I left Vietnam at some future date, I would start with my right foot as a symbol of the end of my journey.

The Vietnamese Army band welcomed us with music. Beautiful girls, called *kongkai*, draped colorful flowers around our necks. For a moment I considered how ironic the greeting was compared to the Marines' departure.

I was in charge of the ammunition unit, based near the beach. Most of the ammo was stored there in case it was hit by a mortar shell and exploded. My unit did not participate in battle, but the danger was always near us and very real. Artillery shells often missed us by a few feet, and we were extremely vulnerable to enemy attacks while delivering supplies to the troops.

A few days passed and I eagerly approached the commander about teaching Tae Kwon Do. He happily accepted and said he had been searching for a suitable soldier to instruct the troops. At first, my students were limited to Korean armed forces, but later, American and Vietnamese soldiers, as well as people from the local villages, joined my classes. Although my language skills were limited, I poured my heart and soul into teaching those students. For them, learning self-defense could make the difference between life and death on the battlefield.

Poor Soldiers, Brave Hearts

Only a handful of the armed forces believed Korea was involved in the war to protect Vietnam's freedom. The real reasons were to repay the United States for their service during the Korean War and to help stimulate the Korean economy.

We were still poor, even during the war: poor soldiers from a poor country. Compared to the American units, our weapons were outdated and our food rations were inferior. Korean soldiers, including me, swindled supplies from the U.S. units and sold them to the local residents for money.

The staff sergeant and I had our own operation. After we collected our sales we would distribute the cash to the Korean units so they could buy radios and cameras. Sometimes I bought beer or threw parties with my share of the money. I am ashamed to admit I did this; I suppose war brings out the worst in people.

I was not the only one acting out of character. A first lieutenant beat me up one day for no reason, in front of my subordinates. I then went to his sleeping quarters after I had a few drinks. I was carrying a loaded gun. "You and I both came here to fight a war," I said. "You had no right to humiliate me just because you have a higher rank than I do. All I am asking is that you show a basic level of respect toward me and others," I demanded. "Unless we can count on one another, we are fighting a losing battle."

He apologized and I went back to my room to wait for the military police to arrest me for threatening an officer, but they never showed up. The following day the lieutenant acted as if nothing had happened, but he started treating his fellow soldiers with more courtesy.

Faced with Death

I lost several of my friends during the war. One close buddy of mine died in my arms from a gunshot wound. Moments before I lost him he asked for some water, which would accelerate the bleeding. "No," I said. "The medical unit will be here soon. Just hold on."

He begged again, "I know I am going to die. Please fulfill my last wish and give me some water."

I just couldn't do it. My friend died just before the medics arrived. I still question to this day whether I did the right thing.

I witnessed many tragedies like this one, and I, too, had my own close call with death. One afternoon, while we were delivering supplies to the front lines, the jeep in front of mine suddenly exploded and catapulted through the air, bits and pieces landing in the jungle about 30 feet from the road. I knew then that we were sitting ducks in a landmine field. Bullets showered down all around us; we were under an enemy attack. I crawled into a mud puddle for protection. After what seemed like an eternity, the shots stopped. I could hear moaning from a soldier nearby. As I tried to move toward him I noticed that I could not move my leg. It was soaked in blood. I had been shot, and I could feel the pain setting in. Two members of my unit died that day and three others were severely injured.

As I was on my way to the medical facility I thought about my mother and how devastated she would be if she lost a second son in battle. Even if I survived I might not have full use of my leg for the rest of my life. I figured I might as well die if I could not practice Tae Kwon Do any more. When I finally arrived at the M.A.S.H.

unit, friends who had heard the news were already waiting to see how I was doing.

Those were the longest minutes of my life, waiting for the doctor to come back with the x-ray results. The doctor informed me that the shrapnel had not damaged any important areas in my leg so I should be able to fully recover. I was probably the most thankful person on earth at that moment.

I spent a few leisurely months in the hospital. I occupied my time reading letters from students in Korea and watching occasional celebrity performances. I decided not to write to my mother about the injury; I figured it would be better if she did not know.

Scars from Vietnam

A close friend of mine was responsible for taking care of the dead soldiers in Vietnam. As the number of casualties increased he became overwhelmed and asked me for help. I didn't have any special training or desire to do the job, but I knew I couldn't turn him down. He taught me how to wrap the faces of the deceased and take inventory of their belongings when they were brought in. Some days we had as many as 40 bodies to keep track of. Most of them were cremated. The bodies of officers were sent home to their families on request. One disturbing part of the job was seeing the pictures of their mothers, wives, and girlfriends, or letters written by their loved ones hoping that they would return home safely. It was also difficult to find letters written by the dead soldiers to their families and friends, but which they had not yet mailed.

War changed us all. It taught us to suspect everyone, even the Vietnamese women and children. They often wandered into our camps to scavenge through the trash, but sometimes they rapidly transformed into enemy snipers. I regret some of my retaliatory actions against them and believe that a lot of them were sincerely looking for food and not conflict. If I ever have an opportunity to go back and meet the people of Vietnam, I would like to get to know them as human beings. I would like to experience their culture, and I would be grateful to know these people as friends rather than enemies.

Americans in Vietnam

My first encounter with Americans was during the Korean War and now I found myself surrounded by them again. I admired how well provisioned and rich they were. It amazed me that they actually built entire houses of wood, put refrigerators in them, and drank cold beer while listening to music, even if it was just for a couple of nights. On the contrary, Korean soldiers slept outdoors with no access to such housing facilities.

I also envied their composure. Americans seldom panicked and always seemed at ease. I became more acquainted with the U.S. troops while teaching them Tae Kwon Do, but we never had a chance to spend extended periods of time together since they were constantly relocating to new bases. We also could not communicate very well. Despite these obstacles, they always respected me as their martial arts instructor.

An African-American soldier approached me one day and said, "We might have different skin colors, but we are both minorities, and I am so proud of what you do. It makes me feel more confident after meeting you." Although I didn't understand him right away, one of my friends translated his comments so I could comprehend.

Martial arts suddenly had a new meaning; it was larger than ethnic backgrounds and international borders. Even though I earned only $50 a month compared to the $400 the Americans made, I had something they did not have: I had Tae Kwon Do.

America Didn't Lose the Vietnam War

U.S. soldiers were much more cordial than Koreans. Regardless of rank, Americans hung out together and drank beer in their spare time. They treated each other with dignity and a kindness that really touched my heart.

But it was a separate incident that really changed my perspective about their culture. While I was driving through the jungle near our base, I heard a loud explosion. I quickly sensed that someone had triggered a landmine. When I located the area where the sound came from, I discovered an American soldier lying on the ground. He was still alive but both of his legs were gone. I moved toward him to help, but when he saw me he painfully turned his torso to wave me away. Instantly I realized I was standing in the middle of a landmine field and he was trying to prevent me from coming any closer. I jumped in the jeep and drove as fast as I could back to base to report the situation.

A few days later I went to see him at the hospital. He thanked me for my help, but I felt I was the one who should be thankful. I bowed my head to him for his courage and thoughtfulness and promised myself that I would someday go to America.

Some 230,000 U.S. soldiers lost their lives during the Vietnam War and although America lost the battle, they won a new level of respect from people like me. Americans transformed our views: we no longer saw them just as people from a wealthy country; we saw them as people from a country that values freedom and individuality.

Today, when I want to remind myself of Vietnam, of that soldier who saved my life, of the chaos, and of the sounds from the helicopters, I buy a Hamm's beer and drink it lukewarm, just like we did in Vietnam. That is enough to take me back to that experience of no refrigerators, no fancy sleeping quarters, no luxuries. We were just soldiers, surrounded by an unforgiving world.

Chapter 8

Returning to Korea and Getting Married

An entire year had passed and it was time for me to go home. On my way back, I asked myself if I had found what I was looking for in Vietnam. I didn't know. I wondered if I had the same look in my eyes that the Marines had when they boarded the ship a year earlier.

As I walked down the gangway I started with my injured right foot first, just as I had promised myself many months before. We arrived in Busan early in the morning, and no family or friends were there to welcome us home. That wasn't our only disappointment. The customs office would not let us bring the televisions and other electronics we had purchased in Vietnam into Korea. Evidently, a local television manufacturer filed a complaint with the government about the overabundance of foreign merchandise coming from Vietnam. The government decided that only officers could bring across televisions; the rest of the equipment would be confiscated by customs. We protested the policy, but it didn't matter. Hundreds of us smashed our new television sets to pieces on the pier.

As soon as I got through customs, I flagged down a taxi and asked the driver to take me to a local bar. I ordered a glass of rice wine and slowly let the alcohol dissolve the pent-up emotions inside me from a year at war.

Thoughts of Suicide

I had sent my entire salary and the money I made selling supplies in Vietnam to a close friend of mine in Korea to keep until I returned. I was sure I had saved enough to pay for the remaining four semesters of college. I was wrong. My friend had invested the money in a business venture that failed and all of it was gone. I was crushed, my gut ached, and I was penniless again.

I became a floater. I slept at one friend's house a few nights and then another buddy's place the next. Soon I was not welcome anywhere and had to sleep in the park. I was filthy and homeless. I washed my clothes in a stream near the park and sat naked until they dried. To make my hunger pain go away, I drank from the stream until I was full. After sunset, I would put my damp clothes back on and look for a place to sleep for the night. I felt hopeless. After three months of feeling like a complete waste, I considered killing myself. It still puzzles me today why I did not, but I am grateful that I faced the overwhelming difficulties and persevered through these challenges.

A Life of Selling

Luckily for me, I ran into an old friend I had met while learning Tae Kwon Do years earlier. He encouraged me and helped me get a job as an insurance salesman. The company we worked for provided us with enough money for a one-way bus pass each day. If we didn't sell anything there was no money to cover our bus fare home. It was one of the toughest jobs I ever had. I met with countless numbers of people, trying to persuade them to buy insurance from me. I learned a very valuable lesson while selling that I often share with young people: if you want to learn about life, you must go out and sell.

I could not make enough money to cover my college tuition and after agonizing over it for days, I finally asked my oldest brother for help. As soon as he heard from me he left for Seoul to deliver the money. I knew he didn't have any extra cash, and later I found out that he had sold a patch of family farmland to cover my expenses.

I paid for my tuition and opened a small tire shop with the remaining money, working as a repairman during the day and becoming a student at night. Thanks to the local trucking companies and factories, business was good. After I had saved enough money from the shop, I bought two taxis, one on an installment plan and the other from a friend who needed to pay off his debts.

I soon discovered that the taxi business was more complicated than I expected. Because of a government-mandated curfew, my taxis were required to be off the streets between midnight and 4 a.m. Also, some days the taxi drivers earned good money and other days they barely broke even. They blamed their financial losses on their customers or on tire repairs that day. Between the curfew restrictions and the constant complaints from my drivers, my management of the business became very difficult. The whole business ended up being a money-losing experience.

One day, I came back from school to find the tire shop completely empty, and I learned that my employees had been arrested. When I arrived at the police station and identified myself as the owner, the officers put me behind bars and released my staff. I was told that I was being accused of selling defective tires for use on a passenger bus, that had caused a major traffic accident that day. I knew that some bus drivers were selling the good tires they had purchased from my shop and replacing them with faulty ones, but regardless of their behavior, the bus company was blaming me for the disaster.

I tried explaining the situation and pleaded my innocence, but no one listened. The police were only interested in the pay-off they were receiving from the bus company and didn't care about the truth. I was locked up for three days, during which I had no rights or respect. I felt completely helpless and disappointed. Even though I knew this type of thing happened all the time, I just couldn't get over it.

Unfortunately, my bad luck had just begun. One of my taxi drivers hit an 18-year-old girl and she had to be rushed to the hospital to have both of her legs amputated. My driver didn't have enough money to settle the lawsuit and ended up going to prison.

I felt terrible about the whole disaster, and especially for the girl and her family. She had been working in Seoul and was trying to support her family when this happened.

A few days later, I arrived at the shop to find the taxi driver's wife and children waiting to plead with me to help get their dad out of prison. If that wasn't enough, on the same night the injured girl's father showed up at the shop drunk and threatened me. It was too much, and I decided to sell both taxis and the tire shop to cover the cost of the damages. Additionally, I also had to borrow money from other people to pay for the lawsuit.

Now, I was not only broke, but I was in debt and had to find a way to repay what I owed. Two years had slipped by since I returned from Vietnam, and I was beginning to think I would never succeed in Korea.

Another Beginning: Getting Married

In February 1971, I graduated from college and married Mira, whom I had met in a very nontraditional way. At that time most marriages were arranged by parents or matchmakers who specialized in "selling the family tree." It was important to know about a family's background, who they were, how they earned a living, if they were hardworking, honorable, rich or poor. Many couples met for the first time on their wedding day, but Mira and I broke that tradition.

Since my father was dead, I had to be the one to take the initiative if I was going to get married, so I had a friend introduce us. We got to know each other over several months. When we got married Mira and I were unsure where our final destination would be. I knew there was more in life awaiting us, but I didn't know if we could leave everything familiar to us behind. Unfortunately, this wasn't the last time I presented Mira with such extreme uncertainty.

Despite all of our obstacles, I have never regretted our choices, and Mira has stood by my side through the good and the bad for 30 years. She maintained our home and raised our children while I chased after my American dream.

Chapter 9

Coming to America

After the taxi disaster I lost all faith in Korea and focused on finding a way out of the country. I wanted to go to America, the land of opportunity, where anyone, regardless of money or power, could be successful if they worked hard enough. I was determined to get there and I knew the timing was right.

The U.S. government had invested so many resources into Vietnam that they desperately needed immigrants with special skills to fill the void. My engineering background met the qualifications and I was able to apply for a visa. Just as I thought the application process was going smoothly, it hit a brick wall. One of the Korean employees at the U.S. embassy rejected my paperwork for no legitimate reason. I asked him what the problem was, but he couldn't provide me with any valid answers. I figured he was looking for a bribe like some government employees I'd heard about, those who wouldn't do anything unless they received a favor in return.

I called the man before he got off work and invited him to meet me for drinks at a fancy bar. When he showed up he wasn't alone; he brought a group of co-workers with him. After a few cocktails he smiled and handed me the passport with an approved visa inside. I was really angry, figuring it was all a setup. I swallowed my anger and worried about the next problem: paying the bill.

Before the embassy people showed up I had asked the owner of the bar to place orders only for items that were the least expensive on the menu. I also told her that I wouldn't be able to pay her that night, but I would repay her as soon as I could and would leave my passport as collateral. She agreed to the offer. In those days, getting a visa to America was like winning a jackpot.

A few days later, I had borrowed enough money to cover the party I threw at the bar, and I went to pay the owner back. She refused and handed the passport to me. "I make a living selling drinks to those guys from the embassy," she said. "They are jerks for putting you through all this, and I want you to go to America and make it big."

Tears rolled down my face as I tried to find the words to thank her properly. Before I could leave, she slipped two ten-dollar bills in my hand. I cried all the way home. I wanted to leave Korea to get away from the corruption, but I knew I would miss people like her, who were incredibly compassionate and caring.

But the bar owner's good deed wasn't enough to make me stay, and I left for America on December 29, 1971. My family and friends had hoped I would wait until after New Year's Eve to leave, but I wanted to welcome 1972 in a new world. I purchased a Northwest Airlines ticket on a three-year installment plan, said goodbye to my new bride, and left Korea to conquer an unknown place.

$35 in My Pocket

I felt alone as I waited in the boarding area. I was about to go to a strange country where I knew no one. My thoughts were interrupted as I heard the attendant call my seat number and I slowly got up to drag myself to the boarding line. I thought, these might be the last steps I take in my native country. I felt both excited and sad at the same time. I knelt down and kissed the land one final time before I boarded the airplane.

Soon after we departed, the flight attendants served us meals. I was anxious to see what kind of food it would be, for I had never eaten on a plane before. The food was great and I ate almost all of it, except for the contents in a small, plastic container. I asked an elderly Korean woman sitting next to me if she knew what it was, but she didn't. I looked around and saw the container open on one of the American's trays, so I unsealed mine. Apparently, it contained powdered milk. I put it to my mouth and swallowed it down in one gulp. About half an hour later, I was headed to the bathroom with the worst case of diarrhea in my life.

After spending half the flight in the restroom, I learned that the powdered milk was actually creamer for coffee. Just as I thought I might collapse from dehydration, the captain announced we were approaching Los Angeles.

My wobbly legs slowly carried me down the steps from the plane, where I stepped on U.S. soil for the first time in my life. I reached back and put my hand in my pocket to make sure I still had my wallet, which contained all that I owned: $35.

Part 3: Survival Game in Iowa

Chapter 10

Iowa, Under Snow

My next flight was scheduled to land in Iowa, where I was meeting my friend Young Bok Kim. I met Young Bok while I was running my tire shop and he was working for the City of Seoul's Revenue Department as a tax collector. During his visits we became friends, and we discussed our dreams of America. Young Bok was studying to work in the poultry industry; his job would involve sorting male and female chickens. When he told me that he would be making decent money, I considered taking some classes too. Then I found out how expensive the classes were, and I gave up the idea.

Before Young Bok left for the States he told me to make sure I came to visit him in Iowa. According to his letters, he was working near a town called Cedar Rapids. Regardless of his invitation, I was worried whether he would welcome me when I arrived.

Before landing in Cedar Rapids, the plane had to make an emergency stop somewhere between Los Angeles and Iowa due to a heavy snow storm. I had no idea where I was. I showed my friend's address to an airport employee and tried to find out whether I was in the right place. He was having a difficult time understanding me and said, "Snow" and pointed at the sky. I realized then that the storm had delayed the plane and I went to sit near the other passengers.

By the time my plane flew into Cedar Rapids, the entire city had been blanketed in a beautiful white snow. It was mesmerizing, but my thoughts about the beauty of the snow were quickly interrupted when I realized there was no one there to meet me because the plane was so late. I had to call Young Bok, but trying to use the telephone was almost pointless. The pay phone had buttons on it instead of a dial and I couldn't read the numbers. I stood there and studied the phone for what seemed like an eternity until I finally dialed his number. I was so excited when it started ringing, but my happiness quickly turned to despair when no one answered. I tried several more times but there was still no answer. I panicked. I just stood there, holding the phone in my hands for almost 10 minutes until a passenger from my flight interrupted me.

My fellow passenger must have seen me attempting to communicate with the airline employee earlier, and he offered to help call the number for me. Unfortunately, he too was unsuccessful. After he gave up, the man led me to a car where his wife was waiting for him. The couple gestured for me to get in and I did. At that point, I felt I had no choice but to accept their offer. They drove for a while looking for Young Bok's address while I sat silently in the back seat. I was relieved when the car stopped in front of my friend's apartment complex, but I didn't know how I was going to get in if Young Bok wasn't home. Luckily, the couple found the property manager and they were able to convince him to let me in. I didn't know how to thank them. I asked the gentleman for a business card and bowed many times until the car disappeared.

Once I was in the apartment, I searched for confirmation that it was Young Bok's place. I was concerned that I might have entered someone else's apartment and would be shot for trespassing. To my relief Young Bok's familiar clothes were hanging in the closet. At last I could relax.

When Young Bok got home he greeted me like I was one of his

long lost brothers. I was never so happy to see anybody in my life. After a few days, I went to find the gracious couple who gave me a ride from the airport. I wanted to properly repay them for their generosity. When I found them, they politely refused and told me they were happy to help and hoped my American dream would come true. By their generous act of kindness, my aspiration to come to America was validated that day.

Searching for the Promised Land

A few days later I was on a Greyhound bus headed for Chicago to deliver some immigration documents to Young Bok's attorney. I thought it would be a great opportunity to see more of America and determine where I wanted to live.

At 4 a.m. the bus pulled into the Chicago station and I waited there until the attorney's office opened. The terminal was almost empty, except for a few people checking the pay phones for left-over change. I was surprised to see this in America and realized that even here, there are both wealthy and poor people.

When I delivered the papers to the attorney, I asked him about Chicago and what kinds of jobs people had in the city. Chicago seemed big to me and attracted a variety of people from different ethnic and socioeconomic backgrounds. I spent the morning exploring the downtown area and then boarded a bus for Detroit, Michigan.

While I was in Korea I had met a radio announcer from Detroit. He asked me to look him up when I had a chance and I figured now was the best time to visit. It was a big deal to be a radio announcer in Korea, but he was one in America, and I couldn't wait to hear his voice thunder across the airwaves.

When I arrived in Detroit, I called him from the bus terminal to let him know I was in town. He was thrilled to hear from me, but said he didn't own a car and couldn't pick me up, so I should take a taxi to his apartment. I was shocked that a successful announcer like him couldn't afford a car. I was even more disappointed when the taxi pulled up to his small apartment. I found out that he wasn't an announcer for a big-time station, but instead was an infrequent radio host for a Korean Christian radio program. Even though he stretched the truth about his success, he seemed sincerely happy to see me and did everything in his power to be a gracious host.

I stayed with him for a day and then boarded another bus to Toronto to visit an old college friend of mine. After three weeks, I decided that Toronto wasn't right for me. I was looking for a life-or-death challenge and the city just didn't have it, so I headed back to Iowa.

When I reached the U.S. — Canadian border, the customs officers searched my bags. They stumbled upon a glass jar I had and questioned what it contained. I told them it was pickled squid in a spicy garlic and pepper paste that my friend's sister had made for me. It was one of my favorite Korean dishes. The customs officers insisted that they check it out themselves. I was so irritated with them that I opened the jar and shoved it under their noses. They quickly backed away and motioned for me to close it and told me to get on my way. I suppose they had never smelled anything quite like this type of Korean food.

Cedar Rapids, Iowa

I decided to make Cedar Rapids, Iowa, my new home. The city was surrounded by farms and countryside with a population of about 150,000, and the people there reminded me of the farmers from my hometown. A significant number of factories provided employment, and I already had a friend in the community. Cedar Rapids seemed to be the best fit for me.

I stayed at Young Bok's studio apartment while I looked for a job as a machinist at one of the manufacturing plants. It was extremely tight quarters for two people. Four apartments shared the same bathroom, which always seemed to be occupied. When Young Bok moved into another apartment a few weeks later, I stayed in the studio apartment, jobless and alone in a room furnished with only a bed and a gas range.

When a Korean acquaintance of mine learned that I had a degree in mechanical engineering, she arranged for me to interview with a steel company in the city. Unfortunately, I barely knew any English and she had to translate the entire interview. The plant manager flat out denied me the job. I was told they didn't want to pay a higher salary to a college graduate when they could hire someone else with less education for less money. We tried other factories, too, but the responses were all the same. I told my friend not to inform any more companies about my degree. Who knew that having a college education would be so problematic? I was upset that no one seemed to care how hard I had worked to finish school and get my degree.

After every attempt to get a manufacturing job failed, I took a position as a gas station attendant. My workday began at 6 a.m. and finished at 5 p.m. The neighborhood kids followed me to and from work everyday. I'm sure I looked ridiculous to them, a short Asian man wearing an oversized work uniform, but I didn't care. I finally had a job and I was proud of it.

Little Superman!

The gas station I worked at was a full-service shop. Although I had some basic mechanical experience from college and the tire store, I had never done any engine work. I needed to hold on to this job, but it seemed like the odds were stacked against me. I was an Asian person with limited English skills and no automotive experience. The only thing I could do better than anyone else was hustle about, putting all my energy into my work.

There were four of us working at the shop and we all took turns pumping gas in between repairing cars. A bell rang in the station, letting us know when a customer had pulled up for service. My co-workers would walk slowly outside to greet customers, but I reacted differently. When I heard that bell chime, I dashed out there so fast that I startled other employees and our customers, who weren't expecting to see a small Asian guy running toward them. Sometimes I even had the gas nozzle in my hand before they finished pulling up. The customers liked to joke that I was hiding behind the pumps waiting to surprise them.

While I was pumping gas, I checked the air pressure in all four tires, as well as the engine oil, antifreeze, and windshield wiper fluid. I also cleaned the front and rear windows. I had to be sure that the owner considered me a valuable employee so I could keep this job.

As winter approached, my peers were less and less willing to go outside and pump gas. They preferred to stay inside the shop where it was warm, and I noticed they started experiencing some mild deafness toward the bell. But I still rushed out the door to welcome customers, even when the windchill dropped to 40 degrees below zero. I didn't even think about the frigid temperatures. All I cared about was earning enough money to send to my wife in Korea.

Cedar Rapids was a small enough town that word traveled fast. After about a month of working at the shop, customers started recognizing me for my hard work and even told the gas station owner how lucky he was to have me. More and more people came to the station to have the "Asian pump man" service their car.

Besides pumping gas and checking fluids, I also informed my customers about potential problems with their vehicles and how to fix them. When they scheduled an appointment to have their cars repaired, I would work as fast as I could with no breaks so they could get their vehicles back as quickly as possible.

Two months passed and profits increased. I knew from owning my own shop that the best way to please an owner was to help him make money. Maybe I lacked special skills and spoke poor English, but I could move fast like no one else. Customers and my boss soon acknowledged my speedy work and began calling me "Little Superman."

Hole in My Sole

Often, the biggest challenge for immigrants is overcoming language barriers. Unfortunately for me, I had to learn the hard way several times. One day while I was working at the gas station, a group of teenage boys came in for gas. After I filled up their tank, I told them they owed $20. They insisted that they had only asked for $4 and said they would not pay for my mistake.

I must have misunderstood them and thought they said to fill up instead of just put in $4. The teenagers knew they were getting more than what they allegedly asked for, but they did nothing to stop me from filling the gas tank. I pleaded with them to pay the $20 but they refused. There was nothing I could do but pay the difference myself.

Incidents similar to this one happened a few more times and each time I had to pay for my mistakes. By the third time I knew I was being taken advantage of, so I put the car up on the hoist and drained out all of the gas.

Another one of my responsibilities at the station was washing cars. The owner bought used cars, fixed them up, and then sold them at the shop. Since I had the least amount of experience, cleaning the cars was almost always my chore. I worked so hard washing and cleaning the cars that by the time I was finished, I was extremely wet and tired. The water seeped through the holes in the bottoms of my shoes, making it unbearable to walk during the cold winter months. The hardest part was not letting customers see my frustrations while they sat in their warm cars and demanded their windshields be cleaned. No matter how cold and wet I was, I never revealed my feelings to them.

99-Cent Feast

I earned $200 a month at the gas station. When I got my first paycheck I bought a digital alarm clock with an AM/FM radio and I used the rest of the money to cover my bills. I had the monthly charge for the airplane ticket, $50 for rent, and I sent $50 to my wife in Korea. By the time I paid for a few minor expenses, I only had $20 left to spend. Even then, living on $20 a month was a difficult thing to do. I had to refrain from buying anything unnecessary.

Buying new clothes and shoes was completely out of the question, but I did break down once to get a $3 haircut. The other extravagant thing I did was that on an occasional Friday I would treat myself to Kentucky Fried Chicken's 99-cent meal. It was months before I finally made this one of my weekly rituals.

KFC was located between the gas station and home and every morning and evening I had to walk by the restaurant and inhale the smell of the delicious fried chicken. It was enough to drive a hungry man crazy!

One morning I woke up so sick that I had to stay in bed all day. While I was laying there all I could think about was chicken; I had to get some of that fried chicken. I bolted out of bed, ran to KFC, and ordered the cheapest meal on the menu. I scrambled to a table and ate every scrap, picking every crumb off my plate. I think that was the best meal I ever had and my body never felt better.

After that experience I decided to treat myself to this wonderful food every Friday afternoon. Although the decision was a lavish one, my life became blissful. Sometimes I would lean against a tree near the KFC restaurant and pretend I was waiting for someone. I let the wonderful aroma seep into my nose and pictured myself sitting at a booth, eating the moist, delicious chicken. By Wednesday my mind was abuzz with excitement; there were just two more days until the end of the week. When Friday rolled around I was so delirious my co-workers probably wondered what I was thinking about. At lunchtime I would run to KFC and order the 99-cent meal. As always, it revived my body and soul, and I am sure I will never taste anything better than that Friday lunch meal for the rest of my life.

In 1986, just a few years later, I traveled through China as a member of the U.S. commerce trade delegation and was treated to meals fit for a king, yet nothing compared to the 99-cent meal from Kentucky Fried Chicken. Every December 31st, for the past 30 years, I have visited the same KFC restaurant to remind myself of those hungry and humble years.

Stealing 50 Cents

I had been working at the gas station for a little over three months when Dave, the owner, asked me to join him on vacation. I was totally taken aback by his offer and asked why he wanted to take me when there were other employees who had been working there a lot longer than I had. He explained that revenues had almost doubled since I started working there and he wanted to show his gratitude by giving me a vacation. I could not resist his offer and thanked him for the opportunity.

But the next day I changed my mind and politely declined his invitation. He looked at me with a puzzled face and asked several times why I had decided not to go. Finally, I told him I couldn't afford to miss a week's pay. He smiled and said he would still pay me for working. I was stunned. "Are you okay?" I asked. "I haven't even worked here half a year. I don't understand why you want to take me on vacation and still pay me."

"Your hard work helped my business grow and I want to show my appreciation for it," he said.

I left with Dave on a seven-day fishing trip to Minnesota. We canoed across several lakes during the day and set up camp at night. By the fourth day, when we were fishing on a lake near the Canadian border, I began to feel relaxed for the first time in months. I returned from vacation revitalized and with a new loyalty toward Dave, who had rewarded me generously for my hard work.

During the year I worked at the station, I never once sat down to take a break. My co-workers would call their girlfriends or wives when business was slow, but I would organize toolboxes and clean the floors and ceilings instead. The other employees became irritated with my diligence and showed their disapproval by giving me dirty looks. I knew they thought I was trying to make them look bad, but I felt that hard work was the only way I could keep my job. I started practicing Tae Kwon Do in the shop when it was slow to show them they shouldn't take me lightly. After that, I never got any more unfriendly glares.

Sundays were my only days off and since I had no car or extra money I usually stayed at home. It felt like being in jail for a day, and one Sunday I couldn't take the boredom any longer. I decided to go to work at the gas station. I already had the keys from opening the shop, so I was able to get in with no problems.

Around mid-day Dave drove by and saw the station doors open. He must have thought he was being robbed because he stopped in to check on things. When he saw me, he seemed surprised and asked what I was doing there. I told him I had nothing better to do but work. I could tell from his suspicious look that he didn't believe what I was saying. I reminded him that he should know me well enough to realize that I wouldn't do anything to harm his business.

During the summer months it got so hot I could barely sleep at night and I would wake up too late to eat breakfast in the morning. By the time 10 a.m. rolled around I was famished; all I could do was drool over the candy bars and soft drinks in the vending machine. I always seemed to be 10 cents short from having a cold can of Coke and a chocolate bar.

One Saturday Dave and the others took the day off and I was working alone. I had just finished changing a license plate for a customer and he gave me a 50-cent tip. With the change in my hands and the vending machines in sight, my dream was finally a reality. I debated for a few minutes whether to use the money or not, but I couldn't resist. I had to have a cold Coke and a candy bar.

I felt awful for stealing from Dave, and for a moment I considered a lesson from a novel I had read years earlier about a thief who swindled a loaf of bread and spent the rest of his life paying for his crime. I could almost understand why he did it.

That was the last time I ever stole from anyone. Twenty-five years after the incident I went to see Dave; he was now the owner of a large car dealership in Cedar Rapids. I confessed to him what I had done and offered him an envelope containing $300. He refused to take the money and apologized for not helping me more during those hard times. At last, I had repented for my sins; my mind and spirit felt free.

Family Reunited

It had been five months since I last spoke to my wife in Korea other than by letter. I couldn't afford to make any international calls on my budget, but her most recent letter made for an exception: I was a new father. I was delighted to hear the news, but I felt the pressure to succeed increase, especially now that I must provide for a new family.

I had to call my wife even if it would cripple my funds. I placed a clock beside me to keep track of the time while I was on the phone, and I vowed to myself to tell Mira only what was necessary and make the conversation as brief as possible.

"Honey?" my wife said. It had been so long since I last heard her voice. I was glad I decided to call. "Your brother, Jung Shik, named our son Jea Won. Do you like it? I think it's a nice name," she said.

I thanked her for taking care of our baby without me there, and I started to close the conversation, when she asked if I wanted to see our son. I told Mira I was looking forward to seeing both of them in America, but before I could finish she put Jea Won on the phone. "Jea Won, honey, this is your dad. Say something to him," she said.

My mind was spinning. I wanted to hear my son's voice, but what could a month-old infant say to his father? While all this was going on, the clock was just ticking away. How was I going to pay for this call on my budget? I wouldn't be able to eat my chicken meal for at least a month. My wife's effort to get our son to talk continued, but he didn't make a sound. As a last resort, she started poking at him. She was determined to get him to cry a bit.

"Jea Won, cry, okay? Cry just a little for Daddy," she pleaded. Our son must have been in a good mood because he didn't make a sound.

My wife poked a little harder. "Aaaang," Jae Won cried. Mira got on the phone and said, "Doesn't he have a wonderful voice? He sounds so healthy and strong."

"Yes, he has a great voice," I agreed. "He will be a big guy when he grows up." I looked at the clock again and let out a long sigh. I was doomed.

Mira finally joined me in Iowa ten months after I started working at the gas station. Jea Won had to stay in Korea with my wife's parents while we both worked full-time jobs and saved money. I was going to have to wait to meet my son.

My wife and I decided we could no longer live in the $50 attic room with no bathroom. We moved to a bigger place for $80 a month. We also bought a $200 used car, a 1960 Chevy with over 200,000 miles on it. Even though the car was old, I felt wealthy to be able to buy it. Mira took a job working the second shift at People's Bank as a keypuncher. I dropped her off at 6 p.m., after I finished my job, and then picked her up at midnight. It wasn't very convenient for either of us, but we did what we needed to do to get by.

It was very difficult for us to be separated from our baby, Jea Won. Although we knew he was well cared for and loved by his grandparents, we wanted him to be with us so we could care for him and watch him grow.

I had not yet seen my first-born child, and soon we were awaiting the birth of our second child. We had no health insurance, and our finances were tight. Mira returned to Korea in 1974 to give birth to our second child, a son we named Jea Hong. When she returned to the United States, she brought Jea Won and the new baby with her.

I was very happy to see my wife and children when they got off the airplane. I was actually meeting both of my children for the first time.

Jea Won was two years old. He did not know me, and he had not remembered his mother, so there was a difficult adjustment period for him as a toddler. Everything was new to him, and he missed his grandparents. I still feel badly when I think of how hard this time was for my son.

Mira and I eventually became parents of four children. Our third son, Danny, was born in 1976. Our daughter, Jinny, was born in 1978. We regard raising our children as our greatest joy and accomplishment.

Mira has been pleased by our move to America. Eventually her entire family moved to the United States, including her mother and brothers and sisters and their spouses. Some of her family members settled in Virginia; others live in Iowa.

Mira and I believed that each of our children should learn about their heritage. Each child made several trips to Korea during childhood, even attended school there at times. They were the first U.S. students to attend classes at one Korean elementary school, answering many questions asked by the other students. Some teachers even asked them for English lessons.

One of my friends called me to express surprise when he saw my son in Korea wearing shoes that were in pretty bad condition. In the 1980s in Korea, most families had only one child. The government heavily taxed families with more than one child. These one-child parents sometimes pampered their only child, who wore perfect clothing with famous logos. My son wore a beat-up pair of sneakers and didn't care or notice. My Korean friend actually admired this attitude, and he used it as an example to his own son that shoes and clothes should not be so important.

All four of our children went alone to Korea for at least a year at the time of their second year of college. Each was provided with a one-way ticket but no money. I figured if I gave them a two-way ticket and they were unhappy, they might just come home and not benefit from an extended stay in Korea.

I also arranged jobs for them to have during their year-long stay in Korea. They taught English, but they also attended classes to study Korean language and culture. I wanted them to have good familiarity with their roots.

I kept informed about how well each of my children was doing during their time in Korea. I was more involved in their safety and well-being than they knew at the time, through my contact with friends and relatives there.

It was difficult for us to send each of our children to Korea for a year. I worried a great deal, but I regarded the experience as important for them. I did provide a return ticket after six months, but by that time the adjustment had been made and all was well.

Chapter 11

Cross-country Trip

After 14 months of working at the gas station, I finally quit. It was time to move on, and I needed to find a job that paid more than $200 a month. Opening a Tae Kwon Do gym and teaching martial arts was something I could do best, plus it didn't require a lot of money to start such a business. At the time, Bruce Lee movies were becoming popular and America's interest in martial arts was growing. It would be an ideal time to open a school and capitalize on the free publicity.

While I was trying to sort out the details, I received a phone call from my friend Moon, who had moved to the United States about the same time as I did. He was living in Detroit on a student visa and washing dishes at night to pay for his education. When I told Moon I was thinking of opening a Tae Kwon Do gym, he suggested that we take a trip across the country to find the perfect location. Shortly after our conversation I took $200 from my savings and got on a Greyhound bus bound for Detroit. When I arrived, Moon was waiting for me in his old junker of a car. "Do you think this car will sustain our cross-country trip?" he asked.

"Don't worry, I can fix it if it breaks down," I said.

We stopped by a hardware store and I bought 1/2- and 9/16-inch wrenches. Next, we picked up a bag of rice and two bottles of kimchee from a Korean grocery store, put Moon's electric rice cooker in the trunk, and were ready to take on the world. "Go to all of America!" we shouted.

We drove through Indiana, Kentucky, Mississippi, and Florida looking for martial arts schools, but they weren't easy to find. Back then, there were only about 20 schools, compared to 30,000 today. When there weren't any gyms to visit, we went to free museums and saw other local attractions. Gas was fairly cheap, only 32 cents per gallon, and to cut down on our other expenses we ate hamburgers and slept in the car. It was a tough journey, but we enjoyed each other's company and seeing different parts of the country.

Our skin started to itch after a few days; it was time to take a shower and cook a decent meal. We searched an entire town before we found a motel that fit our budget. Before we checked in, we went to a local butcher shop to buy a pound of pork for the kimchee casserole. By the time we both took long showers and scrubbed our clothes in the bathtub, the food was ready to eat. It was out of this world. While we were contentedly devouring it, someone pounded on the door.

It was the owner and he was furious. "I don't want your business! Just get out of this place!" he snarled. He threw the money that we had paid back at us, and then he stormed off. I guess he had never smelled kimchee casserole before.

We left the motel with a half-eaten bowl of casserole, the rice cooker, and our wet clothes, looking for a place to finish our feast. We settled for a park bench and ate every last bit of the food.

I called my wife occasionally to make sure she was doing all right, and she always reassured me that everything was fine. When I got back, Mira told me that she had been in a bad accident — she had totaled the car and had to be hospitalized for a few days. I felt horrible and selfish for leaving her alone in a strange city.

Fifteen days later, I still hadn't found a suitable location for my first Tae Kwon Do gym. I finally decided it should be in Cedar Rapids, Iowa.

Audience of Three

When I got back from my cross-country adventure, I discovered that our bank account was $15 in the red. I had to find a job quickly and knew I didn't want it to be at the gas station, so I went to see the station owner about collecting severance pay. He apologized and said his company didn't provide any benefits like that. I next went to see Young Bok about a loan to finance my idea of a Tae Kwon Do school, but he said that Iowa was too conservative and he didn't think there was a high enough crime rate to encourage martial arts study. He recommended that I go back to working at the station instead.

I had exhausted all possibilities except one. John, a former co-worker of mine who came from a well-to-do family, now owned a station of his own. When I told him that I wanted to open a Tae Kwon Do school he asked me what Tae Kwon Do was. I explained that it was similar to karate but even better.

"What are you talking about?" he said. "You don't know karate. You don't look that tough!"

Two of John's friends were standing next to him and chimed in, "If you can break two bricks with your bare hand then we will loan you the money and even select the location for you." They found two old, damp bricks that looked harder to break than any bricks I had ever seen before. I had broken bricks in the past at martial arts demonstrations in front of hundreds of people, but these were much heavier and thicker. I was at a crossroads; it was do or die.

I had to either break the bricks or break my hand if I wanted my gym. After much focus and concentration, I struck the bricks with all my might and let out a huge yell. "Wow!" I heard them scream.

I had successfully broken both bricks without injuring myself.

"Unbelievable!"

"Amazing!"

"Oh, my God!"

The three men stared at the broken pieces in awe. They couldn't believe what they had just witnessed. I couldn't either, and looked at my hand again to make sure there weren't any visible signs of injury. Following the demonstration the guys put me in their car and drove me to a realtor. They were much more cordial toward me now and even opened the car door when we arrived at the realtor's office. As soon as we entered, the three of them excitedly described what I had just done. The realtor seemed impressed and showed me a building for $150 a month. It was located in the heart of the city's poorest neighborhood, but I decided to take the offer anyway.

Building a Tae Kwon Do Gym in the "Ghetto"

According to the realtor, the building had been empty for more than three years. It had previously been used as a motorcycle repair shop. Whatever it had once been, it was now a complete wreck. Spider webs hung down from the doorways, a greasy film covered the floor, all of the doors and bathroom sinks were broken, and the walls were cracked. I met with the building owner and asked him not to charge me rent for the first five months while I paid to have it fixed up. He agreed, and seemed happy to have found a tenant who was willing to rent the dilapidated space.

I called everyone I knew for money until I collected $1,300 in loans. Just when I thought I could begin the renovations, I found out that I needed a permit from the City of Cedar Rapids. When I showed up at City Hall, I was told that I had to comply with the city's building codes, which called for two bathrooms, exit doors every 40 feet, etc. I spoke with an electrical inspector who also informed me that I needed to hire a licensed professional to do all the electrical work and it would probably cost around $1,200. I had to find another way, but I had no idea how I was going to install carpet, put up new signs, and start advertising on my budget. I was discouraged.

Deciding to do the work in my own style, I went to a local K-mart store to buy electrical supplies. Although I was far from an expert, I knew enough from school to get the job done. When the electrical inspector came to look at the building he knew immediately that the work had been done by someone other than a professional. "Who did the work?" he asked.

"I am sorry, I don't understand," I replied.

He then pointed at the electrical lines and light fixtures. "Who did this for you?"

I told him again, "I am sorry, but I don't understand."

The inspector finally lost his patience and demanded, "Why can't you understand me all of a sudden? You understood just fine before."

I followed him around with the most apologetic expression I could make and repeated, "I am sorry, I don't understand." He was so mad he swore at me and stomped out of the building. The following day, another inspector came by and showed me where I needed to make some minor changes. He said that I had to install a rail for use by handicapped individuals in the bathroom stall, so I grabbed an old door handle and asked him if that would work. He looked at me for a moment and said that most people use pipe handrails, but the code didn't specifically say what kind to use. He offered to help me put it up.

The next test my building had to pass was the structural review. I knew it was going to be a huge project since the walls were in such awful condition, so I found a construction site and asked the workers if I could use some of their cement. They generously gave me a whole bag and I was able to use it to patch the cracks. My wife and I painted the walls until the early hours of the morning. When we were done, we replaced the motorcycle sign with a handmade banner that read, "Jung's Tae Kwon Do."

A day later, an elderly lady came by the gym and asked, "What do you have for lunch specials today?"

It became clear that people didn't know what Tae Kwon Do was and we needed to do some serious advertising to get the word out. So, I swallowed my pride and added a familiar word under it in small letters, "Karate." Despite all the hassle, the makeshift sign failed to pass the building inspection and had to be taken down anyway.

The Beginning of a Real Challenge

Following the inspections, I was summoned to the Cedar Rapids City Hall for the final verdict. I knew I had become a big headache for the city, but when I got there everyone knew me. It was as if I had obtained some sort of celebrity status, and those who didn't know me just stared at me like I was some sort of green alien.

I bowed 90 degrees in front of the city hall staff and proceeded to make my speech in broken English. "I am here to teach martial arts to the people of this city. I will give them healthy bodies and teach them to respect others. I will also guide youngsters away from illegal drugs and gang activities. I will do everything I can to help this city become better, so please allow me to have my gym."

As soon as I finished my speech, the city hall staff discussed the matter among themselves. A few minutes passed and then they made an announcement that I didn't understand. I crossed my fingers and asked them, "OK or no?"

The same building inspector who had helped me install the handrails smiled and said, "OK!"

I was so happy I shook everyone's hand several times and shouted down the hallway, "I am best!"

I found out later that even the mayor knew who I was. Luckily, he was a Korean War veteran, and he told the others that Koreans are hard-working and kind people. It was thanks to him, Mayor Donald Canney, that I received permission to open my Tae Kwon Do gym. Mayor Canney would go on to win every mayoral election for the next 23 years. Our relationship grew stronger from that day forward and we eventually even became blood brothers.

When I returned to the gym, I put the "Jung's Tae Kwon Do" sign back up and prepared to officially open the doors for business. I knew that the real challenge was about to begin.

Chapter 12

Grand Opening of Jung's Tae Kwon Do Academy

On September 1, 1973, 21 months after I immigrated to Iowa, Jung's Tae Kwon Do Academy opened for business. The place looked more like a cheap warehouse than a Tae Kwon Do school, but to me it was the best gym in town and I was proud of it. The reality was that nothing had been professionally repaired and it showed. The gym was less than 1,000 square feet in size, there weren't any parking spaces, and it was located in a neighborhood commonly referred to at that time as Cedar Rapids' ghetto.

But I had bigger problems to worry about. I had to find students and find them fast. I needed to do some advertising, too, but all of my money was invested in the building. So I improvised and wrote "Tae Kwon Do" in big black letters on a piece of white paper and taped it to the window, hoping that someone would notice. Sadly, I knew deep down that it would take a miracle for that to be noticed.

I carefully put my uniform on, bowed to the Korean and American flags, and prayed. I then practiced a couple of martial arts forms and did some front and side kicks with loud yells, as if there were hundreds of people watching me.

For two long days I practiced by myself in the training room, until one afternoon the door opened and my first student walked in. Dan was a young man who was taking a break from college to earn money. He said he wanted to learn Tae Kwon Do before he went back to school in three months.

I charged Dan $85 for three months and taught him everything I could during our short time together. I first worked on making his arms and legs flexible and strong and improving his mind and spirit. He quickly learned that there was a lot more to martial arts than just fighting.

During that time, I added three more students. They were the same guys who helped me finance the gym — John and his two friends. I didn't charge them to join since it was through their help that I even had a Tae Kwon Do school. Together, the four of us practiced into the late evening hours, even after classes were officially over. I thought if the place looked busy all the time more people would stop in.

John and his friends turned into walking advertisements for Jung's Tae Kwon Do Academy. They called everyone they knew and told them how excellent the classes were at my school. After two months, word of mouth spread and I had 11 new students.

Break or It's My Head

I didn't have any extra money to do formal advertising, so I had to come up with a creative way to promote the gym. I decided it would be by breaking bricks. It was the perfect way to distinguish my school from the others. I used bricks instead of wooden boards to show the superiority of Tae Kwon Do over other styles, and because bricks were just plain less expensive. It really troubled me that so many people didn't know what Tae Kwon Do was, and I was determined to make my students proud of what they were learning.

I performed the brick-breaking demonstrations only on testing days. They were an example of the power of Tae Kwon Do. "This martial art provides you with a mental toughness that makes impossible tasks possible," I explained. "Please do not imitate what I am about to do or you are likely to seriously injure yourself and then you might decide to sue me," I said jokingly.

With these words, I broke two cement blocks with my forehead. Everyone was shocked; all they could do was congratulate me with a thundering applause. I increased the number of bricks every time we had a testing, and as the number of bricks increased so did the number of students applauding. It wasn't too long before word spread and I became a sort of urban legend in Cedar Rapids. It was a story of an Asian martial arts master on Mt. Vernon Road who not only could break six cement bricks with his head, but who could also touch the ceiling with his front kicks.

Although my publicity stunt was working to perfection, I seriously risked injuring myself every time I conducted the performance. One inaccurate maneuver would have put me out of business for good. A doctor was once in the audience and came over to examine my head after I was finished. "Are you okay?" he asked. I said I was and he shook his head in disbelief and told me I was crazy.

However, my celebrity status wasn't always rewarding. A well-to-do family heard about my abilities and invited me to a fancy restaurant for dinner one night. When I arrived they were already eating their meal and the man at the head of the table asked me to show them some Tae Kwon Do moves while they ate. I felt that I had been manipulated into this. I decided to do a demonstration on my terms. With a loud yell, I began a martial arts form and bellowed louder with every kick and punch. The family was so startled they dropped their silverware and sat petrified for the rest of the 20-minute demonstration.

When I finished, the head of the family apologized and said they didn't mean to undermine me; they just wanted to confirm the rumors they had heard.

Regardless of his apology, I didn't feel any better and was still very upset with them for treating me like a jester at the King's court. I was handed an envelope containing $50 and I hesitated for a moment to consider whether I wanted to accept it or not. After the family sincerely apologized some more I decided to take it. I felt badly for behaving as I had; I had even scared the children. They seemed like a caring and genuine family and I forgave them for what they had done.

Local Punks

Despite our efforts to promote the gym, there were still people who didn't know Jung's Tae Kwon Do Academy existed and those who refused to accept its existence. I guess the local punks didn't find any humor in a small Asian guy shouting and jumping around in their neighborhood.

A few weeks after my grand opening, some of these punks started to shoot windows out of my gym with a BB gun. Luckily the plastic bullets didn't hurt anyone, but they did cause the glass to break and I had to file so many insurance claims that the company finally cancelled my policy.

Eventually the assaults escalated. One night after class, six young guys around 18 or 19 years old stopped in while I was preparing for the next lesson. Each of them was holding steel bicycle chains and broken bottles. I asked them politely if I could help them. When no one answered, I asked again, "May I help you?" There was still no response. Then one of them spoke up and said I didn't show them proper respect when they entered the gym. It was obvious that politeness wasn't going to work with these guys, but I had to be careful not to hurt them if I didn't want the police involved or any lawsuits filed against me.

"I am sorry, but what do you want?" I asked. Suddenly, all of them charged at me with steel pipes and swinging chains. They seemed determined to take me out, no matter what the consequences were. I stepped back calmly and grinned. I knew from past experience that guys who are really tough don't hang out in gangs for backup. I just needed to determine which one was the ringleader and neutralize him. I took a few more steps backward and then made a sudden move forward. They all stopped in their tracks and looked at one another. Their actions indicated they didn't know what to do next. I waited to see who would give them the next order.

Once I identified him, I jumped through the air with a flying side kick, knocked him on his back, and put my foot on his throat. Meanwhile, the rest of his clan bolted for the door and it was just the two of us. I added some additional pressure on his throat and made my scariest face ever. "If you come back, I will kill you," I said. (Of course, I had no real intention of actually killing him, but I certainly wanted to frighten him!)

As soon as I released him he whimpered, "Yes, yes, yes," and scrambled to get out the door. For an entire year, every two-to-three weeks, I confronted similar groups until they finally got the point and stopped coming around.

Real Life Sparring

One evening, while I was teaching the last class of the day, a gigantic man walked into the do jang and demanded I fight him. He was at least six feet seven inches tall, and he weighed about 250 pounds. I kept my composure on the outside, but inside I was panicking. My students, on the other hand, were excited that I might beat this guy up, but I was worried about what would happen if I lost this fight. The thought of my students losing respect for me was too much to bear. I had no choice but to face him.

I went into my fighting stance and yelled really loudly, but he didn't react. Most people are taken off guard by such a yell, but he didn't even budge. My mind was in turmoil. I had to find a way out of this potential disaster. I borrowed some time and asked him to come back in 10 minutes after class was over.

My students were getting more and more eager to see me fight, just like Bruce Lee in the movies. I was at a crossroads again: if I beat him I would be declaring war on the entire neighborhood and if I lost I would be a martial arts instructor who couldn't defend himself. Students would cancel their contracts and I would have to close my school. I looked around the room. My students' eyes were twinkling with excitement. If I have to close the doors I might as well win. Once I made my decision I was ready to face the consequences and have the fight of my life.

But soon I was a wreck again. What if I crippled him or worse? Would I spend the rest of my life in jail and who would take care of my wife and Jea Won?

I asked one of my students to get a pen and paper and write up the following agreement for the man to sign. "This is a fair fight between two men and we will not seek any further action after it's over, even if one of us dies."

His eyes bulged and he said, "I don't want to kill you. I just want to fight."

I shook my head and explained, "I am a professional and need to make sure I don't go to jail even if something happens to you during this fight. If you refuse to sign this paper then I will have to call the police and have them witness this." He just stood there motionless and silent. "Call the police," I commanded.

"No, no, no," the guy said as he slowly backed out of the gym.

That was the smartest decision I ever made. After that first year, I never had any more problems. The neighborhood was still a high-crime area, but it was quiet and peaceful around my Tae

At the service station where I was first employed in Cedar Rapids, between the business's co-owners Gary Junge (left) and Dave Ballstaedt. I worked from six a.m. until evening, except on Sunday when the business was closed.

The Kentucky Fried Chicken restaurant where I purchased a 99-cent meal each Friday in my early days in the U.S., part of my twenty-dollar monthly food budget. Several times each year I go back to that restaurant to reflect and acknowledge the value of humble beginnings and continuing humility.

Instructor, Jung's Tae Kwon Do Academy, Cedar Rapids, Iowa, USA.

Jung's Tae Kwon Do Academy's first location, which opened in 1973 in Cedar Rapids, Iowa. The first sign said only "Tae Kwon Do," which was virtually unknown in the United States at the time. I changed the sign to read "Tae Kwon Do Karate" after several people stopped in to order lunch, mistaking my business for a Chinese restaurant.

Brick-breaking demonstration. I presented Tae Kwon Do demonstrations involving techniques never seen live before in many areas of the United States, such as breaking bricks with my head. Such techniques were amazing to observers and generated interest in martial arts; it was a marketing technique which helped me to establish my successful Tae Kwon Do school.

Flying side kick. This photograph was taken by an amateur photographer in 1975 and was used in advertising Jung's Tae Kwon Do Academy. About seventy photographs were taken at this session, with the inexperienced photographer having difficulty timing the photos correctly. He suggested that I stay in position. I had to remind him that I could not hover in midair!

I always welcomed a diverse group of students at Jung's Tae Kwon Do Academy. Ages six to sixty, all races and ethnic backgrounds, handicapped students: all were welcome. I often gave free lessons and uniforms to children who could not afford to pay to attend.

The first New Life Fitness Center/Jung's Tae Kwon Do Academy during construction prior to opening for business in 1980. Students' donations and their assistance during construction helped me toward the fulfillment of my dream for a new facility.

Although the first fitness facility was nearing completion, I was interested in implementing a new concept, an ice room. I rented a jackhammer and installed the ice room, the first of its kind at a fitness center in the United States.

Winter classes sometimes involve a "snow run." When the temperature is below 20 degrees and the ground is covered with snow, students—with adequate preparation—run outside barefoot. This unique training builds the student's self-confidence.

Tae Kwon Do students lined up on the roof as the flag was raised atop the new fitness center/martial arts facility in Cedar Rapids, Iowa, in 1980. The flag-raising was as significant to me as the breaking of a bottle when launching a ship.

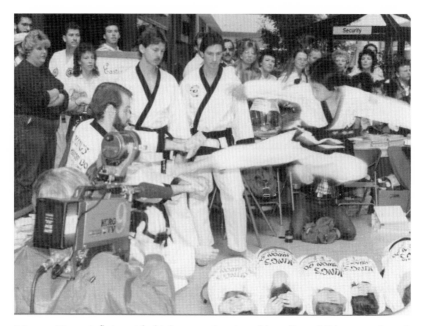

My son Danny's flying side kick over a barrier of kneeling children at a board-breaking marathon. Proceeds from the marathon were donated to charity, in keeping with my philosophy that martial arts should contribute to society.

Mayor Donald Canney spoke at a ceremony commemorating the sister city relationship between Ulsan, South Korea, and Cedar Rapids, Iowa. Mayor Canney and I pursued the establishment of a cultural exchange between the sister cities. Later, our cooperative efforts led PMX Industries, which began in South Korea, to establish a multi-million dollar plant in Cedar Rapids.

Instructors and students are barefoot in the snow at a Friday black belt class at Jung's Tae Kwon Do Academy.

During the early years of the first New Life Fitness World facility there was an expansion, followed by a ribbon-cutting ceremony, nearly every year.

A traditional fighting game of Korea, depicting battles between neighbors a thousand years ago. I arranged this Korean festival in Iowa City.

The 1986 ribbon-cutting ceremony at the Iowa City location of New Life Fitness World included the mayor of Iowa City and former Governor of Iowa, Robert Ray, pictured in the photo below with my wife and me. The Iowa City facility incorporated the size and needs of a complete health club, with no further expansion necessary.

New Life Fitness World, Iowa City, Iowa.

My martial arts journey is depicted in this collage of photographs, showing my progression from young Tae Kwon Do student to Tae Kwon Do instructor and business owner.

Demonstrating an "apple kick,' a fun way to show the skill and self-control attained through martial arts study.

Speaking at a 2000 seminar for students majoring in Tae Kwon Do at Gea Myung University in Deegu, Korea. I enjoy sharing my knowledge and experience with young people.

At the twenty-five-year anniversary of Jung's Tae Kwon Do Academy, with Tae Kwon Do's beloved founder General Choi Hong Hi (second from left) and Mayor Donald Canney (second from right).

First Lady Barbara Bush and Chairman Lyu of PMX Industries at ribbon-cutting ceremonies. The PMX plant employs 500 workers. I was involved in negotiations to bring the company to Cedar Rapids.

Tae Kwon Do 'pioneers' who have worked diligently toward the development of Tae Kwon Do in the United States, pictured at PMX Industries.

In 1988 New Life Fitness World expanded to South Carolina, opening this 33,000 square foot facility in Columbia. I had heard about the lack of fitness facilities in the area and knew this presented a wonderful opportunity. The distance between the Iowa and South Carolina locations of the company is about 1600 miles, but I was excited by the challenge. The stone visible on the outer walls is limestone brought in from Stone City in Iowa; I wanted to bring something unique from Iowa to the facility.

The second Columbia, South Carolina, New Life Fitness World opened in 1989, with health club members participating in the ground-breaking. As at the previously constructed facilities, the sign in front of the building heralds the time and temperature, and the American flag is proudly flown.

Telephone station for members' free usage, furnished at each New Life Fitness World facility. I believe attention to detail is important.

Purchase of a two-engine, eight-passenger private plane enabled New Life Fitness World personnel to travel at less expense than on commercial airliners. However, security measures became very strict and time-consuming for this type of private aircraft, and the airplane was eventually sold.

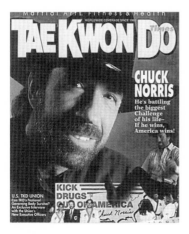

In 1980, Master Chung Kim, Dr. Yang Ahn and I founded *Tae Kwon Do Times* magazine, with famed actor/martial artist Chuck Norris on the first cover of the new publication. The magazine is now distributed in 120 nations worldwide and contributes to the fulfillment of my dream of peace and unity through Tae Kwon Do, connecting martial artists from around the world.

Doing some cleanup work prior to carpet installation at a new facility. I enjoy getting involved in many fundamental tasks associated with the construction of my facilities.

My wife Mira and I have blended Korean traditions into our life in the United States. Here we celebrate New Year's Day with our children. This day was traditionally for family time, with children informing parents of their goals for the New Year.

The United States Small Business Administration named me Iowa Minority Small Business Person of the Year in 1986.

I was honored by this proclamation declaring a 'Mr. Jung Day' in 1990 in Cedar Rapids.

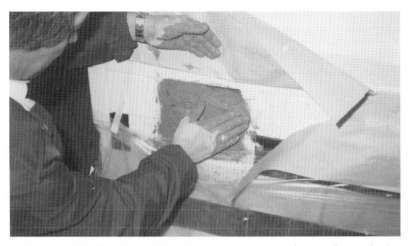

I enjoy providing hands-on labor during construction of a new fitness facility. When some outlets were installed incorrectly at one new facility, I moved the outlets myself, to save time and money. But when members of the labor union questioned who had completed the work, I suggested that perhaps a 'monster' of some sort had entered the building during the night!

I wear the same pair of shoes from start to finish during construction of a new health club. When the building is completed I enjoy 'retiring' the old pair by purchasing new shoes!

I rented a steamroller for this parking lot repair. My Tae Kwon Do background has instilled in me a belief that I can accomplish any task through confidence and perseverance.

Although blind, Dave Oberhart fully participated in all aspects of Tae Kwon Do class, including board-breaking and free-sparring. He attained the rank of black belt.

Black belt Nancy Rowell Stewart demonstrates a beautiful high front kick, while balanced on her crutches. As her instructor, I modified techniques of Tae Kwon Do to allow her to fully train. She later opened a Tae Kwon Do school.

On North Korea's famous Gum Kang Mountain, fulfilling my dream to practice Tae Kwon Do there, imbuing my spirit with the mountain's spirit. I visited this mountain accompanied only by a tour guide. It is a treasured memory.

Business team from Eastern Iowa who traveled to China in 1986 for the purpose of economic development.

I co-own the Eagles Nest with several other martial arts leaders. It is at an elevation of 9500 feet, atop one of Colorado's majestic Rocky Mountains. The Eagles Nest provides a Research and Peace Center where martial artists gather for training and education, and to work together in endeavors to promote martial arts. Pictured in front of the log Eagles Nest are instructors from Jung's Tae Kwon Do Academy. The construction of this eight-sided building incorporated elements from Eastern and Western cultures. It offers beautiful and comfortable quarters, providing respite to those who stay there.

Leading a July 1997 black belt test at 12,000 feet elevation in the Rocky Mountains. The low oxygen level made the test difficult. There was a light snow cover and no vegetation at this high altitude.

Students on a mountaintop close to the Eagles Nest in Colorado. From a nearby mountain, I led them in a workout including free-sparring, forms and one-step sparring.

General Choi Hong Hi is in the center of this photo, seated next to me, at a meeting held at the Eagles Nest in an attempt to arrange for him to visit South Korea to pay homage at the graves of his parents. General Choi was banished from South Korea in 1972, wrongly labeled a communist. A non-political man of peace, he was seen by those who knew him well as a Nelson Mandela—type of figure. He promoted Tae Kwon Do diligently until his death in 2002. He was never allowed a return visit to South Korea.

New Life Fitness World's Ironman Triathalon held in Iowa City, Iowa. The event's contributions benefited charity.

New Life Fitness World offers an array of fitness choices to its members. Pictured here are just some of the many options, such as swimming pool and spa, martial arts and aerobics classes, state-of-the-art fitness equipment, and racquetball.

Enjoying the tournament success of my sons, from left, Johnny (Jea Won), Jea (Jea Hong), and Danny.

A gift from General Choi Hong Hi, founder of Tae Kwon Do. This framed calligraphy is nearly five feet tall and hangs in my office. General Choi completed only one or two of these each year. I treasure this gift, through which General Choi conveyed his confidence in me: he states that I am a man of principle who keeps my word and wants to do the right thing.

With my wife, three sons, and daughter, on the occasion of Jinny's wedding day. From left are Mira, Jinny Jung McCalley, me, Danny, Johnny, and Jea. Jinny married Rod McCalley in May 2000. I am now a proud grandfather of Mia McCalley, born April 12, 2004.

The office staff at New Life Fitness World completing a barefoot snow run to benefit breast cancer research.

At the annual Jung's Tae Kwon Do Academy tournament, making a donation to the area's DARE program. For 26 years the proceeds from these tournaments have been donated to worthy causes.

A dream fulfilled

Grandmaster sees country's best in C.R.

By Mark Sonka
Gazette sportswriter

To the thousands of participants and fans attending the National AAU Tae Kwon Do Championships next week, the four-day jump, punch, and kick extravaganza offers evidence of the sport's booming worldwide popularity.

But to Woo Jin Jung, 57, grandmaster of tae kwon do at New Life Fitness World in Cedar Rapids, it means much more. It's personal.

It marks the fulfillment of a lifelong dream.

Although he is not affiliated with AAU — the athletics organization that sanctions the tournament Wednesday through Saturday at the Five

Seasons Center — Jung, more than anyone else, is responsible for bringing the art of tae kwon do to Cedar Rapids.

It was Jung who opened Cedar Rapids' first martial arts school in 1973. It was Jung who mentored more than 140,000 students the past 26 years, including an astonishing 2,700 black belts. It was

To Jung and his disciples numbering in the thousands, tae kwon do is more than just a sport. It is a way of life in a fast-paced society where computers have replaced old-fashioned manual labor.

Jung who built what became the largest tae kwon do academy in the world.

"In this area, maybe even the entire Midwest, there would be no martial arts without grandmaster Jung," said Guy Smith, a black belt trained by Jung who now works with him at New Life. "He is it. He brought it here. You talk to any black belt, they came through him. The other schools that have cropped up since then, most if not all of the instructors came through him."

Little did Jung know that by opening his tiny school on Mount Vernon Road — the one customers initially con-

■ Turn to 4C: **Jung**

Woo Jin Jung
He brought tae kwon do to Cedar Rapids in 1973.

An article in *The Cedar Rapids Gazette*, just prior to Cedar Rapids' hosting of the 1999 National AAU Tae Kwon Do Championships, recognizing that the scheduling of the AAU Tae Kwon Do tournament event in Cedar Rapids, Iowa, fulfilled one of my dreams.

Kwon Do school, and I was able to continue teaching martial arts without any further interruptions.

I swept the street around the gym, pulled weeds from the sidewalk, greeted people, and paid close attention to the community's needs. The neighborhood was full of teenagers who didn't have any parental guidance. They were getting caught up in gang activities and drug abuse. Most of them lived with one parent or a grandparent and they didn't seem to know right from wrong.

I taught Tae Kwon Do to many of these kids and never charged them a dime. I provided them with free uniforms and loved and respected them when no one else would. From them I learned that the happiest moments in our lives are when we feel accepted by others.

Part 4: Tae Kwon Do

Chapter 13

philosophy of Tae Kwon Do

My life story is inseparable from the lessons I have learned from years of studying the principles of the martial art of Tae Kwon Do. The five basic tenets of Tae Kwon Do are courtesy, integrity, perseverance, self-control, and indomitable spirit. Study of Tae Kwon Do has shaped my life and given me the direction and sense of purpose needed to pursue my goals. I believe martial arts study serves society as a whole and leads to growth of each individual's human spirit.

Martial arts study puts a focus on basic human needs and can be a solution to treating many social ills. Long ago when humans hunted in the wild and relied on their tribes for survival, they didn't have so many of these problems. Today we are surrounded by electronics and other impersonal forms of communication that are not good for the mind, body, and soul. But just like hiking or camping, martial arts can rejuvenate the spirit. Money, age, and physical abilities make no difference in Tae Kwon Do; everything depends on the color of the belt.

People come to learn martial arts for a variety of reasons. Teenagers and individuals with disabilities join to gain self-confidence; others come for exercise and to release stress. It has been medically proven that physical activities are the best way to beat stress. A study also found that practicing martial arts forms can burn as many calories as jogging. Unfortunately, many people find going to a gym extremely inconvenient, but Tae Kwon Do provides an answer to this problem: forms can be practiced anywhere at any time.

Tae Kwon Do also teaches mental strength. A person can break a board when he or she is truly focused on his or her ability to do so. After the board snaps, a sense of self-acceptance and self-respect overcomes the person. There is a feeling of confidence that cannot come from money, prestige, or power.

The world was shocked by the September 11, 2001, terrorist attacks. For the first time, people realized that the United States is not immune to such atrocities, as many had previously believed. As a result, Americans looked to rediscover the meaning of life. Some started going to church again to search for inner peace and the answers to the unexplainable. Some also turned to martial arts, where they could discover for themselves what was important in their lives.

The Heart and Soul of Tae Kwon Do

When I first opened my Tae Kwon Do school I wasn't sure if Americans would accept it. Most of them had never even heard of Tae Kwon Do, but I believed I could win their hearts if I focused on this martial art's unique spiritual aspects rather than its physical components. I knew there was a need for sharing this philosophy after I observed the overwhelming number of societal pressures, economic disparities, divorces and family breakdowns, and crimes.

I believe there are too many obstacles for our children to combat every day, so they sometimes turn to gangs or drugs for support. Some teens even experience mental breakdowns, and, yet society hasn't come up with a solution to solving these issues. I believe if we are to resolve this crisis people first need to have healthy minds and bodies. When we run, lift weights, or meditate we feel refreshed and energized. Tae Kwon Do does all of these things, strengthening body and mind, so one can fight the everyday battles without drugs and alcohol.

Tae Kwon Do Equals Harmony

Tae Kwon Do is an art. When a person accepts it into his life he will experience an inner peace and ability to achieve new mental and physical strengths. *Tae* means feet, *Kwon* means hands, and *Do* means the way. Through the use of his hands and feet he achieves the way, or high mental state.

During class, students run, jump, kick, and yell just like their ancestors did thousands of years ago. Research has shown that Tae Kwon Do stimulates the brain unlike any other physical activity, and increases participants' abilities to excel at other sports that they might not have been able to do before. It is favored by many for its intensity and incorporation of lower body movements, relying heavily on the legs and feet.

When students enter the *do jang*, or gym, they are to respect the "Do," other students, their master, and themselves. I teach my students to bow to the American and Korean flags, their elders, and their instructor. Additionally, students should turn away from their master and the flags when they need to readjust their uniforms.

I have taught my students to focus on the mental benefits of martial arts. During classes, students are instructed to forget about any distractions, family, and work, and instead focus on the power of the mind and body as one. My students have respected my teaching philosophy, but even if they had not understood, I would not have changed what I believe in most.

Chapter 14

Appreciation of Tae Kwon Do

After months of practice, my students began noticing small changes in their lives outside of the training hall. The most notable was a new sense of inner peace that is unique to students of Tae Kwon Do.

These life-altering changes originate from the basis of martial arts: order, respect, harmony, discipline, and meditation. These basics raise a series of questions such as: Who am I? What is the meaning of my life? Searching for answers to questions like these opens the door for individuals to develop into better human beings.

Tae Kwon Do also establishes a sense of belonging. Americans generally value their privacy, but in martial arts they become part of a family. The respect they are required to demonstrate toward their elders and fellow classmates makes martial arts one of the most humble and kind communities to belong to.

Over the years, I have witnessed numerous occasions when families joined Tae Kwon Do together. When a father and son practiced in the same class they would become closer and rediscover the meaning of their relationship. In the past, I have sometimes asked parents to join their child in class; once they experienced the joy of martial arts they signed up to take lessons too. Together parents and children make a great team and encourage one another to attend classes regularly.

The number of students enrolled at Jung's Tae Kwon Do Academy increased over time, providing me with an opportunity to get to know a variety of people from many different backgrounds. I had students who were high-ranking government officials, successful businesspeople, bankers, college students, and people with disabilities. Regardless of their profession or abilities, each one of my students was as valuable to me as my own children. As these relationships developed, so did my love for martial arts.

Tae Kwon Do Instead of Drugs

Jung's Tae Kwon Do Academy was located in the middle of a poor area of town, where kids with less-than-desirable lives ran the neighborhood. Many of them were school drop-outs, and they had parents who were alcoholics or drug addicts. About six months after my school opened, a kid came in to see me. He said he wanted to learn martial arts, but he couldn't afford to pay for classes. His father was serving time in jail and his mother was an alcoholic. Without hesitation I told him I would teach him for free. I said he was welcome to bring his friends, too. Within a few days he and several of his friends were learning Tae Kwon Do. I had students like him, who sought me out, as well as a few I sought out in return.

I had them do odd jobs around the gym to pay for their classes. I wanted them to feel worthy by earning their lessons, and I tried to treat them with the same respect and kindness as I did my other students. Sometimes I think I even treated them better, but I had to keep it a secret to protect them from any jealousy in class.

Unfortunately, I was once the one to humiliate one of these students. One of the kids wasn't putting forth enough effort during class and I scolded him. "Why aren't you working hard? Do you think I teach you for free for nothing?" As soon as the words slipped out of my mouth I knew I had made a huge mistake. It was too late and the student left the gym crying. I still feel ashamed for what I said, and I have worked to keep these types of arrangements confidential.

Many of these kids were already on drugs at a very young age. John, one of my 17-year-old green belt students, was highly involved with illegal substances. I had no idea and was completely ignorant as to how drugs affected people. One day his father called and asked me to speak with the boy. He explained that John had stopped abusing drugs when he started Tae Kwon Do, but now he was using them again.

I had no clue how to handle this situation, but I told him I would speak to John. I didn't know what the result of our conversation would be, but I took a shot at it anyway.

I met with John. "I want your life to be productive and I know you are aware that taking drugs is not the way to have a good life," I said. "I want you to give me all the drugs you currently have with you."

The boy looked at me and handed over all the drugs he had. I assured him that I wouldn't tell anyone about this incident, but he needed to promise me he would never take drugs again.

I paid more attention to him after that, like parents do with their weaker children. Today, John is a successful 40-year-old father who brings his kids to Tae Kwon Do class.

James was another student of mine from a broken family. A member of a gang, this 14-year-old was one of the boys who shattered my windows with a BB gun. I tried to recruit James off the street several times, but each time he declined my offer. Finally, he agreed to come to the gym. When he got there I gave him a quick initial Tae Kwon Do lesson and asked him to break a board in front of the other students. He felt so good after breaking the board that he decided to learn Tae Kwon Do too.

James opened up to me while he was studying martial arts and told me that he sold drugs in order to take care of his mother. He also said he had been to jail twice. Gradually, he started turning his life around; he stopped selling drugs and started working. When he earned his brown belt, James got a second job, got married, and went back to school.

I am so proud of him and how he used the discipline of martial arts to live a better life. James is now a grandfather and brings his grandchildren to martial arts classes. He has also committed his life to helping troubled teens get a new start.

Like John and James, many of my students changed their lives for the better. Eventually they went back to school, got jobs, and looked after their parents. It has been very rewarding for me to be able to help others. I believe their success stories have been brought about as a result of practicing martial arts. I have tried to live my life by these same principles. I hope that I have been the modest and humble person that I have taught my students to be.

Chapter 15

Tae Kwon Do Today — New Challenges

Tae Kwon Do in the 21st century is often referred to as "family style," but this new genre of teaching has presented the martial arts community with a different set of challenges and opportunities.

Most of the bullying, hard contact, and misconduct have disappeared from the training halls, but so has the ability to teach self-defense at a deeper level. Many activities in class have become too light or are no contact at all, and students of all ranks are developing little knowledge of practical applications of the art.

Family-style martial arts will continue to grow despite its competition with more sports-oriented styles and schools. However, it's become even more crucial for instructors to understand the new demands and environment in which they are teaching.

Family style has opened the doors for children, older men, and women. Kids aged 12 and under are the largest group practicing in schools across the country. While they have incredible amounts of energy, they also require constant encouragement, reminders, and reviewing of techniques. They are also less interested in forms, stretching, self-defense, terminology, and tradition.

One obstacle for children is transportation. Since most of them are too young to drive they are at the mercy of someone else to bring them to class, usually their parents. As a result, kids make it to class less often than older students. Instructors need to develop programs with these challenges in mind and continue to instill discipline and the traditional aspects of Tae Kwon Do.

It is also true that when children are properly motivated they progress quite well. I have noticed that children do listen, and the instructor's message does get through to them. I have seen many former students in their late teenage years and early twenties who remember almost verbatim the lessons I taught them as kids. To see these students become outstanding young men and women makes the added efforts involved in their instruction worthwhile.

Adults, on the other hand, have an entirely different set of needs. Most adults who join martial arts are interested in learning real self-defense or are looking for a way to get into shape. Many young men and women are interested mostly in sparring, full contact, full gear, and lack an interest in Tae Kwon Do traditions. Older adults want to understand the traditional aspects of Tae Kwon Do, want to feel confident about defending themselves, and want to enjoy being part of a group.

Family style has combined these differing groups into one class, making it fun and exciting for each participant. Children learn the same stretches that revitalize the adults, and adults run, jump, and kick in the air as if they were kids again. All students work as a team, encouraging and helping each other during class, which results in a bond between young and old that transcends from a class to a family.

Ninety-nine percent of Tae Kwon Do students today will not qualify for the Olympics, compete in full-contact matches, or get involved in other venues. However, these same students will benefit from the attitude, discipline, and respect that Tae Kwon Do develops. Tae Kwon Do training encourages students to be productive, goal-oriented members of today's society.

Part 5: Journeying Back

Chapter 16

Lost Visas and the Senator Who Cared

A s Jung's Tae Kwon Do Academy grew, so did my desire to take my students to South Korea. I wanted them to experience firsthand the culture and the birthplace of Tae Kwon Do. When I learned that the cities of Busan and Ulsan were planning to co-sponsor the first Korean–American Tae Kwon Do tournament in May 1981, I couldn't pass up the opportunity.

I carefully selected five female and ten male students to go. The delegation of 15 students included one of my first Tae Kwon Do students, John Becker; an assistant attorney general of the state of Iowa, Eric Heintz; a Japanese-American, Akio Ikeda; and Nancy Rowell Stewart, a young physically handicapped woman. There were 17 in our entourage, including Nancy's mother and me.

Before we left, we met with the governor of Iowa and the mayor of Cedar Rapids, who presented us with congratulatory letters and keys from the State of Iowa and the City of Cedar Rapids to take with us to South Korea. I was so excited I stayed up nights thinking about our journey and how wonderful it would be to see my family and friends. I even taught the students "Arirang," one of Korea's most beloved folk songs, and I had handmade gifts completed in advance for our new friends in Busan and Ulsan.

Three days before we were scheduled to leave, four passports, including mine, were lost in transit. The overnight courier company said they wouldn't be able to locate them until at least the morning of our departure. I didn't know what to do. Some of my students had scheduled this vacation more than six months earlier and we had people in Korea waiting for us to arrive. We decided to go to the airport in Chicago anyway and we hoped our passports would be there.

But the passports weren't at the airport when we arrived, and I had to send 13 of my students to South Korea without me. Their worried faces troubled me as I watched them board the plane. I felt like a parent sending my children off to war. When the plane departed I called the people in Busan and explained what happened and asked that they take extra good care of my students. I felt terrible about the entire situation.

While we waited for an update from the courier in Chicago, Sandy Akers, one of my students, suggested that we contact a U.S. senator from Iowa to see if he could help. I wondered what a senator could do, but at that point we were desperate for any help we could get. Fifteen minutes after we called the senator's office we received a message from the Chicago passport office. A representative said that the senator's office had called and we would be issued new passports that day.

I was impressed. With the senator's help we were able to get on the next flight to Seoul. Once we landed in Seoul we boarded a second plane to Busan and met the rest of the delegation there. We were so relieved to see each other that we spent several minutes hugging and crying tears of joy.

The Mayor and the Meaning of the Korean Flag

The Busan Civic Stadium displayed a huge banner that said, "The First Annual Korean–American Tae Kwon Do Tournament." Even though it was considered a tournament, our intentions in participating were quite the contrary. We wanted to take this opportunity to build long-lasting friendships between the two countries.

Unfortunately, some of the participants from Busan were more concerned about winning. They were young, strong, and merciless. My students, on the other hand, were not trained for tournament sparring. In fact, I had previously coached them to avoid physical contact with their opponents. Luckily, no one was injured during the competition, but some of my students were beaten up pretty badly. I felt terrible for them, and I was concerned at the direction Tae Kwon Do was heading in Korea. It seemed at the time to be evolving into a mere sport, purely for entertainment purposes.

After the demonstration, we visited the mayor of Busan and presented him with the letters and keys to Iowa and Cedar Rapids. In return, he gave us an appreciation letter for the governor and mayor in Iowa. The gift exchange took most of the seven minutes we were allocated with the mayor, but I wasn't about to just say hello and leave. I asked him to spend more time with us and explain the history of Korea to our delegation. "South Korea should not disappoint students from another country who are studying Tae Kwon Do," I said.

The mayor agreed and spent the next hour discussing martial arts and Korea with us and personally arranged for us to tour the city. While we were with the mayor, I also had one of my students draw the South Korean flag and explain the story behind it. The mayor was very impressed with his flawless explanation and said he had nothing more to add. He even confessed that he wasn't aware of half the information my student had shared.

Chapter 17

Experiencing Korea

Arrangements were made for us to stay at a hotel in Busan, but I requested that we stay with event organizers so that my students could experience Korean culture. It was a great idea, but I didn't realize there would be so many complications.

At the end of the day, I called 14 taxis and sent my students one by one to their hosts' houses. After I sent the last one off, I waited in my hotel room to hear confirmations from each of them. But the phone rang and didn't stop for hours. Some hosts called every two minutes, worrying that their guest had not arrived. After three hours of calls, the last student was finally accounted for. I thought I could get some sleep, but I was mistaken.

I had 10 minutes of peace and then the phone started ringing again. The hosts had all sorts of questions. "What kind of food do they like?" "How should I prepare an egg dish?" "Do I need to get some sausages?" "Can you translate what your student is saying?" "Can I take him out for drinks?" "Is it okay for him to sleep on a traditional Korean bed?" "How many blankets should we give her?"

I tried to advise the hosts to treat them like they would their own children, but the calls continued until 3 a.m., stopped for three hours, and then started back up at 6 a.m. "Would it be okay for me to prepare a Korean breakfast?" "Can I take them to a nearby public bathhouse?" "Do I need both milk and juice?"

Around mid-morning, one of the organizers called, panicking. One of my students was walking around without his shirt on and the organizer's daughter-in-law was completely terrified. I had to get my student on the phone and find out what was going on. "Why aren't you wearing a shirt?" I asked.

"I don't always wear a shirt at home, and you said to act like we do at home," he explained.

"People in Korea don't walk around with their shirts off. You are embarrassing the host family," I said.

He said he was sorry and put his shirt back on. Unfortunately, the mistakes some Koreans made were much more humiliating than my student's error.

Mistakes by Some Koreans

One of the most mortifying experiences in my life occurred while we were in South Korea at the stadium. When we entered the arena, some of the Koreans in attendance started pointing and shouting at my student Nancy, who is physically disabled. "What is that cripple doing here?" they screamed.

Nancy was like a daughter to me and I couldn't bear to hear them patronizing her. The insults were also heard on the street and in restaurants. They wouldn't stop. I was embarrassed and angered by these taunts. I was so upset I couldn't sleep that night, and I was worried that Nancy might have sensed what was being said. I was afraid she would be devastated, but there was little I could do to rectify the problem.

The humiliation didn't stop there. I found Akio Ikeda, my Japanese-American student, who came to the states after marrying an English tutor, crying in a corner. "What's the matter?" I asked him.

Akio explained that some Koreans were looking at him strangely and it was making him feel extremely unwelcome. I quickly realized what was going on. Korea had been under Japan's rule for 35 years and it probably was difficult for many Koreans to understand why a Japanese person would be practicing Korea's national martial art.

I asked Akio, "Who invited you here?"

He pointed at me, "You did."

"That's right. We didn't come here to discuss history, but to demonstrate our love for Tae Kwon Do," I said.

Akio wiped his eyes and said he agreed with me. I still felt awful about what had happened. Despite these uncomfortable occurrences, most Korean people were very kind and gracious to all of us. Likewise, my students were extremely respectful toward Korean customs, and were good about acknowledging the drinking protocols. They accepted cups with two hands from elders, offered drinks in return to those who gave them beverages, and poured glasses with both hands for those who were older than themselves. It made me very proud to be with them in South Korea.

During one of our dinners, about half of my students drank too much. These students were adults, but some of them couldn't handle alcohol in the first place, and after an hour of drinking Soju, one of the strongest Korean rice liquors, they were completely done in. I had to put them in taxis and take them to their hotel rooms myself. The following morning, I jokingly mentioned we should go drinking. A few of them got sick again.

Friendly Hometown Tournament

The city of Ulsan, where I grew up as a teen, sent 10 cars to pick us up in Busan. Each car had huge placards on the front that read, "The First Annual Ulsan Korea vs. America Friendship Tae Kwon Do Tournament." As soon as we entered the expressway, a police motorcade escorted us the rest of the way to Ulsan.

The mayor was waiting to greet us with flowers and music when we arrived and I reciprocated with the letter and key to the City of Cedar Rapids. The warm welcome was very emotional for me, especially since it was the first time I had seen my mother, siblings, and friends in many years. I have always felt close to my extended family and childhood friends, even if much time passes without seeing them.

After we exchanged hugs and greetings, I made a brief announcement to the crowd. "My mother is here today, and I would like to present these flowers to her. Without her I would not be here and could not love Korea so much."

To show our appreciation we opened the bottles of Chivas Regal whiskey we had bought in Chicago. We felt terrible about giving the 30 bottles away when we had hoped to sell them for profit to cover our travel expenses. Several of my students had to work overtime and get second jobs just to help pay for this trip.

At the time, imported products from the United States were in high demand but, unfortunately, no one wanted to buy the Chivas whiskey since it was already available in Korea in 350 ml bottles. Koreans had never seen it in 750 ml containers and said if they purchased it they would have a hard time convincing people it was legitimate.

Overall, the Tae Kwon Do tournament in Ulsan was a more positive experience than the one in Busan. Nancy even participated in a demonstration and broke several boards. I finally felt like we had celebrated a true friendship between Koreans and Americans.

Chapter 18

A Visit Home

When the tournament concluded, we boarded a bus for the village where I grew up. It was the first time I had been back since 1971, when I left home for the United States. As we approached the village I saw a banner that said, "Welcome Woo Jin Jung." The entire community was invited to a party at my old house and we sang and danced to traditional Korean music all day.

That night, I arranged for all of my students to sleep in the house, women in one room and men in the other. Soon after we parted for the night, I started hearing giggling, followed by some other distinctive sounds. Everyone had consumed so many different types of food and liquor that they were experiencing a definite "gastric disturbance." It's still a big joke among us today.

The next morning, I took my students down to the stream for an experience they would never forget. I had them brush their teeth with sand, the same way I did as a boy. While we were there, we helped some village women wash their clothes and had our pictures taken with them. I also took my students to pay respects to my father at his grave. I bowed first, Korean style, and then my students followed suit. I remembered how I cried for days when my father died. I was a young boy then, but now I was grown up, and I thought how proud he would be of his youngest son if he were still alive.

The day slipped away from us, and soon it was time to leave. My students said their good-byes in Korean, just the way I had taught them. My mom presented each of us with a small bag of goodies, like she did with all of her guests. She held my hands for a long time and told me through tears, "Well done, Woo Jin. Have a nice trip back."

Chapter 19

Hungry and Broke in Japan

On our way back, we stopped at Panmunjum, near the 155-mile demilitarized zone. It is the only location where government officials from North and South Korea meet for peace talks. This was our final destination in Korea during our seven-day visit. But there was one more stop we planned to make: Mount Fuji in Japan.

The 17 of us were left with only $1,500 to cover our expenses for the remainder of the trip. The number of suitcases had nearly doubled from all the gifts we received during our stay. With barely enough money to get us home, I started to question whether we should go to Mount Fuji or just return safely to Iowa.

We decided to go to Mount Fuji anyway and boarded a train for Japan. I gave everyone two small bags of cookies and told them that the small amount of food was all we could afford for the rest of the day. A few hours later everyone was drinking water like hippos, trying to relieve their hunger pains.

As if things couldn't get any worse, when we got to Japan we discovered that the mountain was off-limits due to a heavy snowfall. We had to find a cheap hotel for the night, so we went to the local police station to ask if they knew of any. We were thankful when they recommended a couple of inexpensive places, but when we got to our accommodations we found they were far from affordable.

In Korea, rooms were $20 per night, but in Japan they were $20 per person. We were out of options and running out of money.

I couldn't sleep that night and got up at 4 a.m. to go to the 24-hour market. I bought a loaf of bread, ham, sausage, and fruit. The next morning, I gave each of my students a small ham sandwich, half an apple, and half a banana for breakfast. "This is all you get today," I said. "You will have to find a way to eat on your own for the rest of the day. Our goal now is to get home safely."

They stared at me with blank expressions. No one knew what to say. After we finished eating I said, "Well, I'm going to the beach to find some seaweed to eat."

One of my students tried to stop me, "Won't you die if you eat that stuff?"

Akio, my Japan-born student, who was feeling especially bad about the high cost of things in Japan, joined me in my hunt for seaweed. My other students watched us curiously as we ate the unidentifiable sea vegetation; then they finally decided to be daring enough to join us too.

At dinner we went in separate directions for food. Some of us went to restaurants to beg, some gave up on eating and read books instead, and a few managed to make Japanese friends who provided them with dinner.

The next morning we successfully boarded the plane for the United States and returned home safely. While we were waiting at the Chicago O'Hare airport, one of my students found enough money to buy a candy bar and shared it with all of us. When I put the small chunk of chocolate in my mouth I remembered that day at the gas station when I bought a chocolate bar from the vending machine. This tidbit tasted as good now as that chocolate bar did then, but my enjoyment was cut short when I saw how exhausted Nancy was. It hurt me to see her struggling so much.

By the time we got to Iowa, every single one of us was dead-tired and filthy from several days of traveling. We were also very hungry. We went straight to our welcome-home party where the rest of my students cheered our arrival. We gorged ourselves on food. Everyone, including me, was extremely happy to be home.

It is easy to forget luxurious vacations, but one that is full of hardship is memorable. All 17 of us have never forgotten the time we spent in Korea and Japan. We had a lot of fun, but we also endured a level of discomfort that was unknown to many of my students.

Part 6: Into the Health Club Business

Chapter 20

A New Challenge — the Health Club

By the end of the 1970s, Jung's Tae Kwon Do Academy was on fire. More and more students were signing up every day for martial arts lessons. As the numbers increased, so did a dilemma. I was running out of space. The original building was becoming too small to accommodate students and the thousands of people who attended on testing nights. Parking was inadequate. The fire department was also raising concerns about conducting business in a 100-year-old building.

It was time to move, but I wanted more than to just move. I wanted a health club along with a martial arts gym. I knew that a lot of parents who dropped their kids off for class also went to a gym to work out. I thought it would be more convenient if they could have such options all under one roof. It was a great idea, but I didn't have the money to purchase real estate or to pay for a building.

I did know someone who might be able to help. Tate Klemish, one of my students, was also a real estate developer. He and his family all had earned black belts from Jung's Tae Kwon Do Academy, and when I told Tate about my dream to have a martial arts gym and a health club he offered to give me a piece of property. The land was not in the most ideal location, but it was large enough to accommodate both facilities. I thanked Tate for his generosity and told him I would repay him some day for his help.

My next obstacle was to generate enough money to construct the building and purchase equipment for the health club. I visited several banks, but they all rejected me. The banks said that single purpose buildings, such as fitness centers, are high risk and they don't like to approve them. The fact that I was Asian-American wasn't helping the matter either. Most of the bankers didn't even seem to know where Korea was, and perhaps they were concerned that I would pack up and leave the country if my health club failed.

I didn't give up. I continued knocking on doors, but the outcome was always the same until I approached Brenton Bank. I met a young assistant vice president who carefully reviewed my application. He asked me if I had $50,000 in cash, and explained that the total cost of the project was $400,000, which meant the bank required a minimum investment of $120,000. I enthusiastically told him yes, even though I knew I didn't have the money. It was my last hope and I wasn't going to let it slip away.

I had two months to come up with the money. I didn't have a clue where to start, but I was determined to find the $50,000. Out of desperation I did something that no Tae Kwon Do master should ever do: I asked one of my students for a loan. Lynn Sackett and seven members of his family were taking lessons from me. He had recently been injured in a car accident and received a $30,000 settlement payment. Lynn was still in the hospital when I was considering asking him for the money, but when I got to his room I couldn't find the courage to ask. I visited him three more times and each time I failed. On the fourth visit, I went to his house after he had been released. With a long sigh I explained the situation to him and asked if he would loan me the money. I told him that I could only afford to pay interest on the loan for the first year, but I would make sure I repaid all of the money as soon as I could.

Lynn didn't even hesitate; he immediately said yes and loaned me the $30,000. I was able to get the remaining $20,000 from personal friends, and the bank approved me for the building loan. Three years later I repaid Lynn in full with interest.

My Building

A few weeks later the construction process began. I decided that I would do some of the work myself and have a few of my students help in order to save money. Tate Klemish suggested that we do the painting, lay the carpet, and put up the insulation, which accounted for 20 percent of the project. I also used outdoor carpet instead of tile around the pool and put up 2x4s instead of 2x6s for the walls. To help finance the exercise equipment, I sold club memberships at discounted rates before the gym opened. But despite my efforts, there were still a lot of corners I had to cut in order to stay within budget.

I knew my building inside and out by the time it was finished. It was a good thing, too, since the city required me to have an inspector from the Department of Buildings come out to examine it. Ironically, the City of Cedar Rapids sent the same man who inspected my first Tae Kwon Do gym years earlier. We both had to laugh when we saw each other. "I won't give you a hard time today," I said. "And I won't claim I don't understand English, so you can review everything."

"This is your building?" he asked.

I smiled and explained, "If you hadn't let me open the first gym, I wouldn't be here today. I know you gave me a break before, but I'm not going to ask for another one this time." The inspector smiled back and said, "Your business provides jobs and generates tax revenues for the city, which helps the citizens of Cedar Rapids."

The grand opening was one of the happiest days of my life. After six months of hard work the club was ready for business. Two-thirds of the building was allocated for the fitness center and one-third was for the Tae Kwon Do training studio. The facility also had men's and women's locker rooms, a swimming pool, steam room, and dry sauna. On the outside, a cornerstone sign was hung that read, "Jung's Tae Kwon Do Building."

I bought the original building, where the first Tae Kwon Do school was located, and I still use it as a martial arts gym today. I hope to turn it into a Tae Kwon Do library sometime in the future for students and the community to use.

Going Crazy

After opening the club I soon learned that constructing and operating a fitness center were two totally different things. In Korea, there wasn't even a business that resembled this industry — even if there was, it would be too expensive to join. Someone once told me, if you want to fail quickly you should publish a magazine, make a movie, go into mining, or operate a fitness center. I think he may have been right.

The club was open every day from 6 a.m. to 10 p.m., except Christmas Day, and I was the one who opened it in the morning and closed it at night. Despite becoming a slave to my business, the number of members did not increase as I had hoped and I was becoming physically and mentally drained.

I took my first day off in almost a year on Christmas and slept until the early evening hours that night. The only reason I woke up was to eat. I don't think I had ever slept so long and soundly before in my life. Over the next two years, I only took two days off. Mayor Canney saw me one day and said, "You look like a mad man. You really will go crazy if you continue this pace." He said I should take some time off and go on a vacation trip with him. I wanted to go, but I couldn't. I didn't know who would manage the club while I was gone.

"I don't think I should go," I said. "You go on and have a nice time."

"You will die if you don't stop this madness," he said. "Take a few days off and experience living for a change."

After much persistence on his part, I agreed and we went on a four-day fishing trip to Minnesota. The mayor owned a vacation home there and planned for us to participate in the International Ice Fishing Tournament.

The scenery was breathtaking. Everything was entirely on ice. Even the traffic signs were posted on frozen lakes, similar to how they appear on highways. Ice fishing was a fascinating experience for me. I was amazed by how quickly the fish froze and then recovered in warm water.

For the first time in my life I drove a snowmobile. It was an incredible release to be able to yell at the top of my lungs. I screamed anything that came to my mind, things that I hadn't said since I was a child. Half the time I couldn't even understand what I was saying. All I cared about was the beautiful scenery and the rush of the high-speed snowmobile. It was enough to melt away two years of pent-up emotions. It was also the best medicine any doctor could have prescribed.

I thanked Mayor Canney for kindly inviting me to go. He was a generous man with a high degree of integrity; his term in office as Cedar Rapids' mayor was longer than any other mayor in the nation.

Successful Heroes

After a few months of operating the health club, I started to accept my limitations. I understood that while a good Tae Kwon Do master possesses the leadership skills to command and discipline his students, a whole different set of talents is required of a business owner.

Without realizing it, I treated my club members like they were martial arts students. I showed them how to exercise and provided them with all kinds of unwelcome advice. Eventually, membership started to dwindle and I knew I had to do something to save my club. I sought out some advice from a few friends who told me I had to stop acting like a drill sergeant with club members; they were there to enjoy themselves, not to be criticized.

I was dealing with different people who were interested in achieving an entirely different set of goals. People joined health clubs to exercise their bodies, not to achieve mental strength and definitely not to receive free advice from me. Despite my new discovery, membership continued to decrease and my club was on the brink of failure. I had to put every penny I made from the Tae Kwon Do classes into the fitness center.

My staff consisted of one full-time employee, one part-time employee, and me. I was the sales manager, facility custodian, and martial arts instructor. Sandy Akers, who was my full-time staff member, was also a black belt. She had been working with me seven days a week since the club opened and only took Christmas Day off. She was my right-hand person and I relied on her a great deal. I was devastated when she decided to take a new job in St. Louis with a larger health club chain. I knew I couldn't ask her to stay and sacrifice a better-paying job when I couldn't afford to pay her more.

"I am sorry our hard work didn't pay off," I said. "It's my fault for not having a better understanding of the health club industry, but I still have high hopes that this club will succeed." I asked her if she could find a professional manager in St. Louis to help me operate my club.

A few days after Sandy left she called to say she had met someone who was high-energy and the best salesperson in the city. She gave me contact information for this man, whose name was Mike O'Keefe, and I immediately sent him a plane ticket with an offer to come and work for me. He outright rejected my proposal and said he didn't have any intention of moving to a small town like Cedar Rapids.

I didn't give up. I sent him a second plane ticket and told him I would pay for his expenses if he came to visit for the weekend. Reluctantly, Mike accepted my offer. I picked him up from the airport in a limousine and took him to the club. Once we were there, I demonstrated Tae Kwon Do for him and continued to try to persuade him to manage the club. "Isn't it better to be a manager instead of having to take orders from someone else? I would give you full decision-making powers and let you lead as you wish," I said. After a lot of discussion, Mike finally agreed to take the job.

Business turned around after I hired Mike. He was a marketing genius. He designed free weekly passes and distributed them throughout the city. He also had a special knack for signing people up for memberships.

My Partners

Mike O'Keefe worked with me for over 12 years. I still consider him one of the most valuable business partners I've ever had, because he understood the health club business and provided the knowledge I needed at the time.

Another employee who was also a huge asset to the company was Randy Snook. His personality was somewhat the opposite of Mike's. Randy was well-organized and a perfectionist. He had the ability to know what I was thinking just by looking at me. I named him the vice president of business operations and the office manager. Randy was a relentless machine. During the 18 years that he worked with me, he managed all my finances and never once took advantage of me or the company.

I learned that in order to have a successful business, I not only needed to hire competent employees, but I had to pay them more than my competitors would. I felt that as an immigrant, I needed to make my offer more attractive than other club owners who were American. Neither Mike nor Randy worked in my business only for monetary gain, but I made sure they stayed happy financially. Currently, they are both consultants to New Life Fitness World and I hope to continue to show my gratitude toward them for as long as I can.

Chapter 21

Fitness Center to Fitness World

Three years had passed since I first opened the fitness center and I was in need of a second bank loan to finance a building addition. I went to see the loan officer at the bank and politely bowed before him. I knew my credit history had to be pretty good since I always paid my bills and taxes on time.

With no problem, the bank approved me for a Small Business Administration (SBA) loan. This type of loan is guaranteed by the federal government, thereby reducing a bank's financial risk. I heard once that 70 percent of the businesses that receive SBA loans fail, and only 30 percent pay back the money they borrow. I asked why the government continued a program with such high failure rates and was informed that it was because the benefits of new jobs and tax revenues outweighed the costs.

My club did not fail, and the bank approved me for more SBA-guaranteed loans down the road. As a result, the SBA recognized me as Iowa Minority Small Business Person of the Year in 1986. I brushed it off and regretted having to fill out all the paperwork for the award. I felt like I was wasting my time, but other people thought it was a huge deal and congratulated me for it. They even said I should list it on my resume as an accomplishment. I had no idea it was important; I was just trying to survive and was proud to be one of the businesses to overcome the odds. I wished that more people would act on their dreams like I had.

I was able to expand my business in 1982 and 1984. My competitors, on the other hand, were struggling to keep their businesses going due to poor management or other factors. In 1984, when one competitor's business failed, I bought the building and decided to open one of my clubs there.

The former owner of the gym shut his business down on a Saturday and emptied out all of the exercise equipment the following day. The courts weren't open on the weekends, so he was able to flee with all the machines while the creditors watched helplessly. This could only occur in America. In other countries the government would never allow such a thing to happen.

I bought the building the following week, and purchased a second one in 1985 under similar circumstances. In 1986, I built a new health club in Iowa City and changed the name of my business from New Life Fitness Center to New Life Fitness World. As my dream grew so did my ambition to overcome more and more obstacles.

Chapter 22

Lessons Learned

One of my dreams was to expand New Life Fitness World. When I learned that the beautiful metropolitan area of Columbia, South Carolina, was lacking good fitness facilities, I decided to seize this opportunity. Although South Carolina was a great distance from my business home base in Iowa, I saw no need to limit myself geographically. In fact, I welcomed the challenge such an opportunity presented.

In 1988, I sought approval for yet another loan to build a fitness center in Columbia. I knew it wouldn't be easy, especially since the bank had just denied a previous applicant's proposal. I was hoping that since I was experienced in the industry I would have a better chance.

The loan officer asked me for a detailed business plan, including current company information and projections. I had no such proposal prepared and asked the bank representative if he could provide me with a list of consultants who could help me. I ended up hiring a certified public accountant. He collected all sorts of information, such as demographics about the area and the number of local fast food restaurants. He also requested personal information from me such as what kind of work I did, how I dressed on the job, and how my family life was; he even asked about my parents.

I thought he was initiating a personal conversation with me

about my parents, but it was just another component of the plan. He wanted to know about their past work habits. I told him, "My father worked 365 days a year until the day he died, and my mother made our clothes from scratch, using cotton balls. She raised six of my father's siblings plus six of her own children."

He was shocked. "I have never heard of anyone working so hard," he said. "Children of parents who are hard workers tend to work just as hard if not harder."

Although at times his questions felt intrusive, I was impressed by his professionalism and to-the-point attitude. With his help, I was approved by the bank and received the financing I needed to build a fitness center in South Carolina.

I believe the U.S. banking system is the best representative of the American way, fair and equal. I took full advantage of it. When people ask me how to get a bank loan, I tell them a few things I have learned from my experiences. First, if they don't have industry-specific experience, then they must find someone who does. Second, they must be honest; their personal integrity and character are of the utmost importance to the bank. Last, a bank should be considered a life-long partner and a resource to help grow their business. Banks are there to make money, too, but their success depends on their clients. I will admit there were times when I felt I was mistreated because I was an immigrant. But now I know and respect the fairness and thoroughness of our banking system.

Tae Kwon Do Spirit

I dedicated a place in each one of my health clubs to Tae Kwon Do. After all, it was my students who made it possible for me to generate funding for my business endeavors. However, having a martial arts studio and a fitness center under the same roof created some problems for me.

To be a successful Tae Kwon Do master I needed to have a certain degree of authority and respect from my students, but to operate a fitness club I had to be a servant to my customers' needs. My problem wasn't that I didn't understand this, but that I couldn't distinguish between my students and the fitness members.

Sometimes I mistakenly greeted my students with, "Hi. How are you?" This was strange to them since I usually welcomed them with a traditional martial arts hello. Other times I acknowledged club members with, "Pilsung," a Tae Kwon Do greeting that means certain victory in Korean. My enthusiasm often took them off-guard and they reacted unfavorably to me.

Another obstacle I faced was the fact that I am an Asian-American person managing fitness centers in the United States. Some of my members seemed disappointed when they learned I was the owner. I guess this was strange to them.

Despite this, I tried to make my customers as comfortable as possible and kept a low profile when I was in the clubs. I figured if there wasn't a reason for me to be seen, members didn't even need to know I was there.

I am proud of what I have accomplished, especially when most Asian Americans were pigeonholed into opening grocery stores and dry cleaners. I credit the spirit of Tae Kwon Do for my success. I believe in the martial arts philosophy that you don't give up even if you fall 100 times.

It took a lot of persistence and dedication to compete with fitness club owners who questioned my abilities. I turned a deaf ear whenever I heard them say, "What does a martial arts person who drives an old beat-up car know about health clubs? He doesn't even speak English very well."

My response to that is that Tae Kwon Do gave me the mental edge to succeed and persevere even when success seemed impossible.

Cleaning Obsession

The middle school I attended in Korea had a huge banner hanging over the front of the building. It said, "Diligence and Integrity." Those two words were drilled into our heads over and over again. For me, remembering the words wasn't difficult, but living by them was. I made up my mind early on that I would be diligent and maintain my integrity under all circumstances. I wanted to be known as an honest businessperson, not someone who was deceitful and greedy. I even decided I would be content with failure as long as I stayed true to this motto.

Oddly enough, cleaning is the way I have demonstrated my diligence and integrity. Having a clean environment is important to me and my customers. You would never find a McDonald's restaurant anywhere in the world with dirty tables and bathrooms. McDonald's prides itself on cleanliness. Employees are constantly wiping down tables and mopping the floors. I believe this is one of their top ingredients for success and it became one of mine as well.

I became obsessed with cleanliness. My mission was to find the hard-to-reach corners and out-of-sight places that employees overlooked. Because of this, I took on the nickname "Eye of the Eagle." I cleaned vents, urinals, and the backside of toilets until they shined like a soldier's belt buckle. I did all of the dirty work, including scrubbing the inside of the toilet bowls with my hands. It was not a pleasant task, but it had to be done and I was usually the one who did it.

I also became a junk collector. I picked garbage up off the club floors whenever I was walking through my fitness centers. People often thought I spotted money by the way I was so eager to pick an object up. One time, I was walking through with my general manager and we spotted some junk on the floor. I was the faster of the two of us and picked it up while he stood there and pointed it out to me. "There's another one. Here is another," he said. I finally got up and looked at him, "Hey, who is the boss here? You pick it up."

We both started laughing. When there wasn't a garbage can nearby, I deposited the junk into my pants pockets. My friends liked to joke that my pockets contained more garbage than they ever did money.

I did these things because I am not a financial genius or a marketing guru. I love my businesses and want to focus on providing the best customer service I can. I am constantly thinking of ways to serve my club members better. I consider customer service when I'm working, eating, walking, and sometimes while I'm sleeping. I think about it when I'm traveling. I try to put myself inside the customer's head and see things from his or her perspective.

I know I would want a friendly greeting after a long day at work and I ask all my staff to welcome customers with a warm, sincere hello. I also require employees to wear name tags and uniforms. I think soldiers look stronger and police officers look more professional when they're in uniform.

Although I expect these policies to be followed, I am far from obsessing over them. In Korea, we have something called *jung*. It's difficult to translate into English, but it means a strong caring feeling for the people around you. It can be demonstrated as affection, passion, compassion, or hate. You can have *jung* toward people you like as well those you dislike. *Jung* makes Korean people who they are. It's not something that we learn in school, but a feeling we develop as we grow older.

There are many ways I express *jung* toward my employees. Whenever any of them go on vacation I give them a small amount of extra money. It might not be much, but it makes my employees and me feel good. I also pay for my upper management's rental cars or hotel rooms during their trips to remind them that I am successful because of them. Some people might think I do this to make my staff work harder (and sometimes they do), but I do it because I care and consider all of them very important to me.

Above, in 1981, looking from South Korea into North Korea. At left, in 1995, with a group of *Tae Kwon Do Times* delegates, looking from North Korea into South Korea. My dream is that one day the two countries will reunite, forming one country: Korea.

The *Tae Kwon Do Times* group is shown seated on the North side of a meeting table in a building located half in North Korea and half in South Korea. The building is used for meetings and negotiations, and the table itself is divided, half in North Korea and half in South Korea.

At the Tae Kwon Do World Games in North Korea, in 1991. The tournament was considered newsworthy worldwide because it provided some evidence that strides were being made toward a peaceful coexistence between North and South Korea.

The use of this 25-passenger Russian helicopter was provided to our 1995 *Tae Kwon Do Times* entourage by the President of North Korea, Kim Jong Il. We had traveled to North Korea to select property for a Tae Kwon Do sanctuary.

Left, I enjoyed my part in arranging this unprecedented touring event in 1992, when Tae Kwon Do demonstration teams from South Korea and North Korea were brought together to demonstrate martial arts on a tour through the United States. This was one of many steps toward establishing peace and better relations between the U.S., North Korea and South Korea. Below left, an article which announced an upcoming trip to North and South Korea in 1996 by members of the Board of Governors of the Taekwondo World Foundation. The trip was to serve as a diplomatic mission to promote peace, but it was cancelled by South Korea one day prior to departure when a political crisis involving North Korea occurred. Those board members pictured include columnist Jack Anderson, Congressmen Bob Livingston, Toby Roth, Nick Smith, Charles Taylor and Gene Taylor, martial arts pioneer Jhoon Rhee, and me. The cancellation of this trip remains one of my greatest disappointments.

I work with other martial arts leaders to promote martial arts awareness and practice throughout the world. Pictured from left are Master Dave Moon of Mexico, the late ATA President Hang Moon Lee, Tang Soo Do President Jea Chul Shin, me, and Hapkido founder Bong Su Han (back to the camera).

The doors of martial arts are open to those with disabilities. This martial artist, confined to a wheelchair, enjoys a tournament moment with, from left to right, Master Ko, Master Choi, me, and Master Moon.

With ITF President, General Choi Hong Hi, at the 25-year anniversary celebration of Jung's Tae Kwon Do Academy in 1998.

With former WTF President Unyong Kim. Dr. Jung Won Jo is the new WTF President.

With new ITF President Jang Wong, who became ITF President after General Choi's death. I work diligently to get along with both sides in political and Tae Kwon Do matters. I look forward to the day when there is one Korea and one Tae Kwon Do.

I am seated at far left, pictured with my mother (third from left), brothers, and sister.

Jung's Tae Kwon Do Academy black belts Don and Susan Booth and a group of their students from New Horizons Black Belt Academy in Lawrence, Kansas, journeyed to South Korea and paid their respects to my mother on the occasion of her 100th birthday.

This symbolic drawing was presented to me on my sixtieth birthday by my long-time Tae Kwon Do student Robert Wood and his students. The tree's roots are strong as it overcomes challenges. My roots are also strong, and they have provided me with determination and a will to overcome the odds.

Reunited with Hyo Shin Kim, the businessman who paid my college tuition years earlier. I searched for him for 38 years, making phone calls and sending letters. Mr. Kim was given two plaques, one in English and the other in Korean, at a special presentation. This great man assisted many people throughout his generous life.

With family and friends from my hometown at ceremonies in honor of the Korean publication of my autobiography. These lifelong friends chartered a bus to take them to Seoul for the event.

Presenting a Lifetime Achievement Retirement Benefit Award to Master Jhoon Rhee. I established a Grandmaster Honor Society, which each year honors four or five individuals who have contributed to the development of martial arts.

The facility of New Life Fitness World commonly referred to as the "White House," because of its pillars and the white color of the exterior of the building. It opened in January of 2003, the third facility in Columbia, South Carolina. The grand opening was a special day, shared with the construction laborers and their families. They were presented with plaques to recognize their hard work and excellent craftsmanship.

Ground-breaking at New Life Fitness World in Lexington, South Carolina, 2004.

Catch of the day, Alaska, summer 2004. I traveled 11,000 miles on a twelve-day trip to Alaska with friends, driving 192 hours. The journey symbolized a challenge for me, and seeing the beauty of the wilderness of Alaska was a dream come true. Through living according to the tenets of Tae Kwon Do — courtesy, integrity, perseverance, self-control and indomitable spirit—all challenges can be met and all dreams can come true.

Freestyle Sparring, a book I co-authored with Jennifer Lawler. I believe in sharing my Tae Kwon Do knowledge as much as possible, through writing, teaching, and seminars.

The 30-Year Anniversary Autobiography Celebration

Five hundred people waited in the darkened room for the start of the banquet and ceremonies commemorating the 30-year anniversary of the opening of Jung's Tae Kwon Do Academy and the publication of the first printing of my autobiography. I entered the room, carrying a single candle, accompanied by the Neil Diamond version of the patriotic song "Coming to America." I carried $35 in cash and a Tae Kwon Do uniform tied with my much-beloved and worn black belt, symbolic of all that I brought with me when I arrived in the United States in 1971.

My older brother lit a candle to depict the spirit which my family sent with me as I journeyed.

Another elder brother presented me with rice and a Korean flag, to symbolize that throughout my journey my roots would remain with me, never to be forgotten.

Former Mayor Donald Canney presented me with
corn, soybeans and an American flag, symbolizing my
arrival in Iowa and my American citizenship.

John Becker, the first of more than 4000 students to attain the rank
of black belt through Jung's Tae Kwon Do Academy and its satellite
schools, lights a candle to symbolize the light brought into the lives
of Tae Kwon Do students.

A new generation
of Tae Kwon Do
students lights a
candle to symbolize
new dreams and
continued growth.

Rod Speidel, editor of *Tae Kwon
Do Times* magazine, lighting a
candle to acknowledge the
founding and development of
the only Tae Kwon Do magazine
with worldwide circulation.

Candle-lighting by long-time instructors from Jung's Tae Kwon Do Academy.

Candle ceremony participants forming a line at the front of the room. Each symbolized an important aspect of my life. Together we were pioneers. There were family members who helped me immigrate to the United States. There were my early students, and my first black belt student. There were those who helped me in my first days in the fitness business, and those who helped me establish *Tae Kwon Do Times* magazine. There were people I helped to immigrate to the United States, and there were students I assisted in arranging attendance at American colleges and universities. There were business representatives of PMX Industry. Charities which received proceeds from Jung's Tae Kwon Do Academy's tournaments and special events were also represented.

A vase hand-painted with my portrait contains the flags, rice, corn and soybeans. John Becker, the first black belt of Jung's Tae Kwon Do Academy, tied the black belt around the vase.

Speaking to the banquet crowd, thanking my family, my Tae Kwon Do family, and my business friends and associates for their presence at the 30th Anniversary/Autobiography Ceremony. I expressed my gratitude for the help and loyalty given to me by so many people throughout my life, recognizing the contributions of others to the development of my *Eastern spirit* and the achievement of my *Western dreams.*

Sharing a treasured moment with my granddaughter, Mia McCalley, in my office at New Life Fitness World in Cedar Rapids, Iowa, 2004.

Chapter 23

More Lessons Learned

A nother pivotal lesson I learned in business is the importance a location plays in the success or failure of a company. For example, McDonald's restaurants and Walgreen drug stores, two very large franchise companies, are always located near busy intersections in a city.

It is for that reason I consulted area Chambers of Commerce before determining where to build my fitness centers. I gathered useful demographic information, selected a few favorable spots, and then got in my car and drove from one site to the targeted demographic area. If a city had a population of 100,000, then I tried to avoid a driving distance of more than 10 minutes. However, residents living in places where the population is 200,000 or more are usually okay with driving more than 10 minutes to their destination.

Another test I made was to visit the local grocery stores to gauge the financial status of the residents living in the area. Unless my service was tailored to suit the needs of my customers, I was likely to fail.

I also got aerial perspectives of my locations. The city looks so different from a helicopter. It's easier to detect concentrated residential and commercial areas, expressways, and roads.

Once I selected my business location, then the building process was ready to evolve. I put a great deal of consideration into the interior design and how it would appeal to my customers. I learned this in Las Vegas, where businesses decorate their buildings with extravagant bright shimmering lights and vibrant colors. The outcome has subtle positive effects on customers and it keeps them coming back again and again.

I also like to have my customers be involved in the construction process. It is my belief that it's important to invite new fitness members to the groundbreaking ceremony, rather than only inviting politicians or other VIPs. I have the members' pictures taken wearing construction hats and holding plastic shovels to take home as souvenirs. As a result, they leave with a sense of ownership and new attachment to the club before it's even opened for business.

Between Heaven and Hell

I think I might be one of the few people who feels as if he visits heaven and hell on a daily basis. Most successful Tae Kwon Do masters achieve a superhuman-like status among their students. This is common among instructors who earn a great deal of respect and authority from their students, but it's also a dangerous mind-set to maintain. Martial arts masters must be careful not to let it interfere with their teaching philosophy. The respect and good treatment sometimes feels like a bit of heaven though.

As a health club owner, I must also transform my identity into one who treats my clients like they are gods. Some members complain and shout demands about many things, from the temperature in the pool to the type of music that's playing. The gripes triple when any of the exercise equipment is broken down. Being put in a position of having to respond to so many constant demands sometimes feels like a little bit of hell.

Between the martial arts studio and the fitness center, I find myself in heaven and hell every day. It's an interesting challenge.

Failure Makes the Challenge Worthwhile

Most Americans live paycheck to paycheck and, until 1999, I was an employer who struggled to pay my employees on time. At one point, I had to get second and third mortgages on my house and put the first Tae Kwon Do gym up as collateral so I could pay my staff. Some people wondered why I had such a difficult time with the finances since I owned several clubs, but after deducting expenses and taxes I was left with barely enough to survive. A lot of the money also went toward expansion and the construction of new clubs. For the most part I believe I was successful, but my success did not come without bitter failure.

In 1991, I bought out a fitness center in Florida that was previously owned and operated by a dear friend of mine who died of liver cancer. Although I knew the chances of succeeding were small, I paid full price for my friend's business and hoped the money would help his young children and widow.

I did everything in my power to make that business profitable again, but after three years of hardship I had to close the doors. I spent countless nights awake, thinking about how I failed; I just couldn't come to terms with it. But in the end, I have never regretted buying the club for the sake of my friend and his family. Without this failure, success would never taste so sweet.

Part 7: East Meets West

Chapter 24

Respect for Differences

In 1996, I went to China as a representative of a trade delegation organized by the State of Iowa. It was my first visit to the country and I wasn't sure what to expect. When we arrived, the Chinese welcomed us with elaborate dinner receptions, and police motorcades escorted us to events as though we were high-ranking officials. The Chinese encouraged us to build factories, nuclear generators, and dams in their country. We explained to them that we were only there to find future investment opportunities; we were not ready for immediate large endeavors. I suggested they learn English, and I offered to provide them with tutors, but they persisted in talking about building factories.

Despite our language barriers, we were able to return their hospitality by inviting the Chinese delegation to the United States that same winter. When they came to Iowa, they were puzzled to see Americans drinking ice water in the winter. "Why are you drinking ice water when it's so cold outside?" they asked.

"I'm not sure," I said. "Why do you drink hot tea during the summer?"

Each country has its own unique culture; it's just a matter of respecting our differences so we can get past them and understand one another better. Eventually, we will all encounter new cultures, especially during this age of rapid globalization. I believe the experiences I have had in both the East and the West have proven beneficial to me and my businesses.

There was a time when I wanted to expand my company into another country. I guess there are no boundaries to my dreams. But even with my strong desire and drive, starting a business venture outside of the United States was much too difficult. I have received countless inquiries from a number of wealthy investors in Korea and Japan about opening health clubs there. They visited my fitness centers and learned about management and gym equipment — at no cost to them. Many of the investors asked me to either join them as a partner or manage their new facilities. Unfortunately, none of them followed through, even though I supplied them with valuable information that I had collected the hard way.

Chapter 25

Tae Kwon Do Is More Than a Business

I have given Tae Kwon Do lessons to about 160,000 students and close to 4,000 of them have gone on to earn their black belts. I consider each of them a treasure in my life and I am proud to have been their instructor. Currently, Jung's Tae Kwon Do Academy has 7,000 students enrolled in 45 branches in Kansas, Missouri, Ohio, and Iowa. These branches are owned and operated by my students. I do not have a franchise agreement with them and I don't require royalty payments. The business is completely up to them and they are free to make all of the decisions.

Martial arts made me a successful businessperson, making it possible for me to succeed in the fitness industry, and with *Tae Kwon Do Times* magazine, department stores, and real estate opportunities. I feel it's time for me to return some of the profits and pay back to others what has been given to me.

There is one more dream I would like to fulfill before I die. I would like to build martial arts schools for young people across this country, just as former President Jimmy Carter built homes for the poor. I no longer consider Tae Kwon Do a moneymaking business, but I look at it as an incredible experience that I want to share with the world.

Tae Kwon Do Trailblazers

On April 11, 1955, Tae Kwon Do was founded by General Choi

Hong Hi. The general was a leader in South Korea, and he stood firm in his opposition to the Japanese during their occupation. Vicious rumors and lies were later told about him, and his reputation remained damaged for years. General Choi immigrated to Canada after that and continued to devote his life to promoting and educating people about Tae Kwon Do.

General Choi was by nature and by choice an apolitical man. He was devoted to Tae Kwon Do, and he worked diligently to further knowledge and practice of Tae Kwon Do throughout his lifetime. He was most certainly not a communist, but defamatory rumors were spread that he was sympathetic to communism. Despite the difficulties the unfounded rumors created for him, he did not shirk from his mission of promoting Tae Kwon Do throughout the world, even venturing into communist countries to promote his beloved martial art.

On June 15, 2002, at the age of 83, General Choi died. His final wish had been that he would be laid to rest on the Korean Peninsula. Through the Grandmaster Honor Society that I represent, I lobbied both the North and South Korean governments, hoping to obtain an agreement to his last request. But because of the General's history and the bad feelings between the International Tae Kwon Do Federation (ITF), which General Choi founded, and the World Tae Kwon Federation (WTF), the South Korean government denied the proposal. However, the North Korean government did agree that General Choi's last wish could be fulfilled by his burial there. As a result, many South Koreans still believe that General Choi was a communist.

Two men have taken on General Choi's devotion to Tae Kwon Do. Ki Ha Lee, ITF senior vice president, and Kwang Sung Hwang, ITF general secretary, traveled extensively with General Choi through communist countries, including China, Cuba, Russia, North Korea, and many Eastern Bloc nations, to inform people about martial arts. Today, Lee and Hwang are also unwelcome in South Korea. In fact, when the parents of Lee's future bride found out about his status, they terminated the prewedding engagements and broke off the relationship.

Unfortunately, some people have caved into pressures from outside sources and have broken away from the ITF. Despite these internal feuds, General Choi is the undisputed father of Tae Kwon Do and true martial artists will recognize his standing and continue to stay loyal to him.

Tae Kwon Do was first introduced to Americans during the 1970s. The martial arts community divided into two major branches: The American Tae Kwon Do Association (ATA) and the American Tae Kwon Do Federation (ATF). ATA consisted of 25 Tae Kwon Do masters and was exclusively for martial arts professionals who were also known as purists. Those who had backgrounds in judo, Tae Kwon Do, and other martial arts belonged to the ATF. Both organizations formed to provide support to their members and to spread Tae Kwon Do across America.

There were many turf wars that broke out between the newly founded Tae Kwon Do gyms and existing martial arts schools. In fact, it was not uncommon for Tae Kwon Do masters to get into physical fights with instructors from other martial arts gyms. One case in particular was the Japanese Yakusa. The Yakusa tightly controlled Hawaii until the late 1970s and when Tae Kwon Do masters attempted to open schools in their neighborhoods, the Yakusa had them killed. As a result, we lost four martial arts instructors during those brutal battles. Two of them, Kyo Woon Lee and Dave Kim, are still remembered today for their honor and commitment to spread knowledge and study of Tae Kwon Do.

Unfortunately, it was also not uncommon for the ATA and ATF to have major disputes as well. One day, a wife of a good friend of mine, Master Min (who was also a member of the ATF), called me crying. She said her husband had been beaten and bloodied the night before during a fight. I immediately went to his house to hear his explanation of what had happened. Evidently, Master Kim, a member of the ATA, had a gym near Master Min's new school and had been threatening him for some time, attempting to force him to leave the area. Master Min told Master Kim that no one had such rights and he would not move out of the neighborhood. So, Master Kim sent some of his students to Master Min's gym to beat him up.

A few of us got together after this happened and demanded that the ATA issue a formal apology to Master Min. When the ATA refused, we decided we would confront them after a scheduled ATA tournament in South Bend, Indiana. About 25 of us met in Chicago and drove the rest of the way together. We were all well aware of the seriousness of this fight, including Master Min, who asked me to take care of his family if anything should happen to him.

Before Master Min immigrated to the United States, he was part of the Korean military's Special Forces. We knew that he was not afraid of sacrificing his life for a worthy cause, and he was not afraid of killing anyone either. Because of this, we felt it was our responsibility to prevent him from doing anything drastic to the ATA members.

Unbeknown to us, an ATA member's wife called the police when she saw us arrive. We confronted the ATA members and demanded an apology. Just as we expected, they refused and we started to prepare for the biggest fight of our lives. But before we could even throw one punch, four truckloads of SWAT officers surrounded the premises.

I am relieved that nothing happened that night. If it had, I have no doubt that it would have been one of the most tragic moments in Tae Kwon Do history.

Chapter 26

Visit to North Korea

In 1992, the North Korean government invited me, as the publisher of *Tae Kwon Do Times* magazine, to attend the World Tae Kwon Do Federation tournament. The invitation read, "We believe Master Jung is one of the top Korean nationalists who has worked for the Korean people and for national peace."

I couldn't refuse their offer and decided to go even when some of my friends tried to convince me otherwise. They said the country was too dangerous and they were worried that something terrible might happen to me. Their point was well taken. North Korea is still one of the few communist countries in the world and is under control of a strict dictator. I reassured my friends that it was just one of many Tae Kwon Do events I would attend.

I first had to make a stop at the North Korean Embassy in Beijing to obtain a visa for entrance into the country. When I arrived, a North Korean consul came out to greet me.

"Mr. Jung, thank you for helping the North Korean Tae Kwon Do delegation get U.S. visas," he said.

I had previously invited 15 North Korean delegates to attend one of the martial arts tournaments in the United States. I explained to him, "I am a student of Tae Kwon Do and operate a small school in Iowa. Anyone could have done the same."

The consul insisted that he escort me to the airport and promised to take care of all my travel arrangements while I was there. His eagerness to accommodate me helped relieve some of my anxieties about the trip.

I boarded the plane for Pyongyang, the capitol of North Korea, the next morning. Since the war, the two Koreas have been divided at the 38th parallel for almost 50 years. It was emotional for me to see any part of North Korea. I was surprised that the flight attendant even allowed me to take pictures through the airplane windows.

When the plane landed I started worrying again. My life was now in the hands of a dictator who had shown little regard for people outside his country. I stayed seated until the rest of the passengers exited the plane and the stewardess came back to my seat. I asked her, "Do you think it's safe for me to get off this airplane?"

She smiled and said, "There is nothing to be worried about."

Although I wasn't completely convinced, I had no choice but to exit the plane too. Once I got off, I found the North Korean guide who would be taking me around during my stay. When we entered the airport, the news media surrounded me. I didn't want the trip to turn into a political campaign. "I am not here to play politics," I said. "If that is what you are trying to do then I would like to go back right now."

Almost immediately the guide said, "Reporters, stop!"

And, like magic, they disappeared. He then led me to the VIP room where he asked for my passport. I started to get nervous again when I saw I was the only one in the room. He next took me out to the parking lot where there were several tour buses and taxis waiting. I walked over to a bus, but the guide stopped me, pointed to a Mercedes Benz automobile and said to get in. I was getting uneasy; I simply came to observe a Tae Kwon Do tournament. I didn't think I deserved such accommodating treatment.

Before the guide dropped me off at the hotel, he took me to see the huge statue of Kim Il Sung, the North Korean dictator, at Monument Park. The statue towered over me; it also gleamed so much that I thought it must be polished regularly.

When we got to the hotel, I tried to pay for the room, but the guide interrupted me and explained that during my visit to North Korea all of my expenses would be taken care of.

It was now after dinner, and I needed to let my family know I was okay. I wrote them a message that said, "I arrived safely, so don't worry too much."

Just as I was about to fax it, I saw a disturbed look on the guide's face. I asked him for another sheet of paper and rewrote the message to say, "I was warmly welcomed by the North Korean government and they have taken care of everything, including my meals and nice hotel room."

When he saw the note he smiled and said, "This is a wonderful message."

I suppose his work performance included my comments about him as well. By this time I was more at ease and jokingly commented, "When I was young, people told me that North Koreans all had red eyes because they were communists."

He snickered and stretched his eyes wide open with his fingers. "Take a look. Are they red? No, right?" He then said, "Mr. Jung, you are in your homeland. Relax and enjoy your stay. We will do whatever is necessary to make your visit pleasant."

I asked him, "Why are you going out of your way for me? I am only a Tae Kwon Do instructor from a small town."

"Mr. Jung," he said, "you are working to bring peace to the two Koreas through martial arts. We are grateful for what you are trying to do."

People of North Korea

The North Koreans treated me like royalty while I was there. I was especially amazed by my visit with Kim Il Sung, North

Korea's dictator. As a South Korean, I never dreamed I would meet him, and I had a strong preconceived notion of what he might be like. I was surprised to find him very personable in my one-to-one encounter with him. He grabbed my hand with both of his and told me, "Thank you for coming so far, Mr. Jung."

My second-eldest brother was killed in the Korean War, and I have felt his loss my entire life. I am not sympathetic to communism. It is important to me that I remain in an apolitical position, though, so that I can better work toward the goal of world peace that is so important to me.

Koreans have suffered far-reaching consequences because of the division of Korea. Families have been divided, and not allowed contact with each other for all these years. Such a forced separation of loved ones has been emotionally painful to many Koreans.

Maintaining the division of Korea at the 38th Parallel has proven to be very costly financially as well. Military forces from both North Korea and South Korea police their respective sides of the division at all times.

Kim Il Sung passed away a few years after our meeting, so I never had a chance to visit him again. He left a strong impression on me during our brief encounter, because I saw a personal side of him that was not evident in his public appearances.

One other memorable moment that occurred during my trip was while I was sharing a cab with a few other U.S. attendees. Through casual conversation with the taxi driver we learned that he and another passenger served in the North and South Korean armies respectively at the same time near the DMZ. The driver asked him, "Are you the one who was playing that propaganda music so loud that it kept me up all night?" I couldn't help but laugh, and felt happy and sad at the same time. That was my first of a number of visits to North Korea.

Chapter 27

One Korea

Tae Kwon Do has taught me to look beyond unimportant barriers. I believe that all students of martial arts should embrace each other regardless of where they are from. One way for me to minimize the distance between North and South Korea was to build a Tae Kwon Do Sanctuary in the North.

In September 1995, an attorney specializing in international law, a group of Tae Kwon Do masters, and I all went to scout out a few potential sites for a sanctuary. We were provided with a 25-person helicopter, made in Russia, to fly us to our destinations. On board, there were seven of us from the U.S. Tae Kwon Do delegation, four from North Korea, four representatives from the construction industry, and two flight attendants.

The helicopter had a long table in the middle with benches on both sides; also present were two North Korean soldiers armed with guns. The presence of weapons made all of us very uneasy. After a few minutes, I offered one of the soldiers a cigarette and said, "Try a cigarette from the U.S. You might like it."

He refused. I lit the cigarette anyway and offered it to him again. "Go on, taste it."

He reluctantly accepted it and took a couple puffs. "Tastes good," he said.

I put the whole pack up to his face and told him to have them.

He looked surprised, took the pack, and thanked me. I turned to one of the flight attendants and asked her, "Do you have anything to eat? I am kind of hungry."

"Yes! We have lots of snacks," she said. Almost immediately she brought us beer and all kinds of other refreshments. After having a few drinks we all started to relax and I asked the soldiers if they could take off their guns. "You are making us all very uneasy carrying them around," I explained.

"Oh, I'm sorry," one of them said, and they both took their weapons off.

Now that I felt a little more confident I asked if I could try on one of their hats. One of the soldiers took off his military hat and handed it over to me. We took pictures of me wearing the hat, and we sang old Korean folk songs. For a moment, there were no guns, no boundaries, and no politics to divide us; we were all just Korean people with one culture and one heritage.

Once we arrived at our destination, the soldiers put their guns back on and we became quiet and serious. I was surprised to see a Cadillac waiting for us and asked them, "Why do you have an American-made car?"

One of them explained, "Americans often come here, and they like it when they see one of their own cars."

The other soldier stopped by a handbag store on the way through the airport. I overheard him mumble, "My daughter would love to have that bag." I took him into the store and bought the purse for his daughter. Moments later, the rest of the North Korean delegation was in the store wishing for handbags, too, and I ended up buying them all gifts. They were very happy and appreciative of my gesture and excited to give their wives and daughters the presents.

Soon after we left the airport we found the future site of the Tae Kwon Do Sanctuary. I shook hands with everyone and said, "For the next 100 years, this is the new home for millions of those who love Tae Kwon Do. Congratulations, everyone!"

Building the center would be an enormous task. I hoped I could fulfill my own expectation of helping the two Koreas become one. Someday I hoped my homeland would unify as one country, referred to without division: Korea.

Three Countries, One Goal

Tae Kwon Do has touched the lives of millions of people worldwide. It has brought self-discipline, respect, kindness, and competence to those who have chosen to embrace its culture. It has provided a foundation upon which I built my family. It has been a school to educate students and a business to support my family, but it has also been a source of hope. There is hope that after countless unsuccessful peace talks, the two separate Korean countries can reunite and resolve their long-time differences.

Since 1972, the two Koreas have agreed that unification should be achieved peacefully. Unfortunately, it has been a very difficult goal for many North and South Korean leaders to reach. The DMZ is still a way of life in the Koreas, separating an estimated 10 million families and stagnating fiscal growth, agriculture, trade, and culture.

But one very strong tie remains between the two: martial arts. In 1985, the Korean governments' first attempt to improve relations was made by initiating cultural exchanges and sponsoring single teams to represent both Koreas in international sports competitions. In 1988, the United States followed suit and began facilitating athletic, cultural, and scholarly exchanges with North Korea.

As a native South Korean and citizen of the United States, reunification of North and South Korea has been important to me and to my family. I strongly believe that Tae Kwon Do can facilitate peace between the two countries. That is why in 1995 a group of

Tae Kwon Do masters and I decided to form the Tae Kwon Do World Foundation, a nonprofit organization that included former Speaker of the House of Representatives Bob Livingston, Congressman Tom Foley, former Secretary of Agriculture Mike Espy, Washington Post columnist Jack Anderson, and movie star Chuck Norris.

Together we initiated a trip to North Korea in 1996, and we began organizing martial arts demonstrations for the next eight months in New York, Chicago, Los Angeles, San Francisco, Houston, and Seattle. Our plan was to fly to Panmunjom and hold a board-breaking demonstration, and then travel to Seoul. The journey would end with a visit to the president of South Korea. We sent letters to both governments stating our intentions and asked if they would be willing to accept our offer.

Suddenly, three months after the three governments agreed to participate in the tour, South Korea backed out. It was unclear to me why after so many months of planning, the South Korean government changed its mind. The U.S. State Department told us that a North Korean MiG jet had defected into South Korea and increased tensions between the two countries so they could not guarantee our safety if we proceeded with the trip. I also later learned from an individual representing the Korean Consulate in Chicago that many South Korean government officials were experiencing pressures from outside sources who wanted to dissolve the country's commitment to the tour.

I was devastated and depressed for days. I still have all the materials we prepared for the event: brochures, books, and banners. It saddens me to know that I was not able to successfully see the Tae Kwon Do tour through. It was my hope that this exchange would help facilitate a peace agreement among the three countries, all of which still share the same goal: reunification of the two Koreas.

Chapter 28

My Endless Challenge

S ome might say I made it big in America, and I would agree with them to a certain extent. I am still not sure why I have succeeded, but I would like to think it has to do with how I have lived my life. Some people have even asked me what I'm going to do with my money when I die. "You know, you can't take it with you," they say.

I have been criticized for not spending money like other people. I know some things are essential, like owning a car, but it took me 16 years after immigrating to this country before I bought a good car. I drove an old junker before that and fixed it myself when it needed to be repaired. My wife and I bought a small house 18 years ago, and we still live in it today. I wear casual shirts, dress pants, and gym shoes wherever I go. Last year, for the first time in my life, I bought a pair of dress shoes.

I thank the American people for teaching me how to live a frugal life. I have tried to absorb only the good aspects of this culture and so far I believe I have done a good job. My Tae Kwon Do schools, health clubs, and tree nursery businesses are all designed to make people feel better. Nice clothes and expensive cars don't make people happy. I feel truly blessed to have had the opportunity to dedicate my life to others.

I have also had my ups and downs throughout the years. In 1973, soon after I opened my first martial arts school, I suffered from a horrible gum infection and couldn't eat or sleep for several days. I finally went to see a dentist. After the exam the dentist looked at me sympathetically and asked, "Do you have dental insurance?"

"No," I said.

He referred me to a Korean dentist at the University of Iowa's School of Dentistry. He was trying to help me cut down on the costs of my dental work and make it easier for me to communicate with a dentist. I was very appreciative of his referral.

Several students took turns examining and treating me at the university. At first I was impressed by all of the attention I was getting, but I found out later that the professor merely used me as a guinea pig so his students could gain practical experience. As a result, the inexperienced students cut off most of my gums and I still suffer from the treatment today. I am sure a lot of immigrants have gone through similar experiences, and I now know that if this were to happen to anyone else there would have been a lawsuit.

Unfamiliarity with the English language also created a lot of barriers for me. It took me many years before I could communicate my thoughts with minimal difficulty. My deficiency in English was especially problematic when my students' parents came to me for advice. I often struggled to articulate what I wanted to say, losing what I intended to communicate in the translation. Some of the time my words came out too blunt and students didn't understand what I was saying. Because of this, I truly value and envy those who can communicate well with others.

Remembering U.S. holidays was another difficult task for me. Unlike Korea, where celebrations fall on the same dates, many American holidays vary from year to year. This new system confused me for the first few years that I lived here. I worked on most of those holidays out of pure ignorance, but the most embarrassing incident was when I sent my son Jea Won to school, only to find out classes were canceled and he had to walk back home in the cold, wintry weather.

I made all kinds of mistakes during the first five years I lived here, but all of these experiences made me feel even more grateful when I received my U.S. citizenship.

The Joy of Sharing

One component of U.S. culture that truly impresses me is Americans' willingness to give and volunteer. People give their hard-earned money to worthy causes and happily help others who are less fortunate than they are, with no expectation of receiving something in return.

Some Americans even donate their life savings to the community and leave very little to their children. Traditionally, Koreans leave everything to their children and if a family tries to give their wealth to society their kids protest the decision. I believe that giving back to the community shows your children how much you love and respect them. I have decided to give much that I have back to society, and thankfully, my family understands my intentions.

Americans share more than their money. When they get a driver's license they have the option of donating their organs to others. I think it's wonderful to be able to save someone else's life when I die. I once saw an advertisement in Korea for a company that pays for organs. It amazes me that this occurs even in Korea, where the culture does not approve of such a practice.

Another example of how loving people are in the United States is highlighted by the adoption process. Many Americans adopt children regardless of race, color, sex, or physical or mental abilities. Once they adopt a child they treat the adopted child the same as their biological children. Unfortunately, Korea has not yet implemented a good adoption process. There are still many abandoned children. For the most part, Koreans don't believe in adoption and feel their children must have their own bloodline. Most couples would rather seek surrogate parents than adopt. As a result, a lot of Korean children are sent to the United States so they can be adopted by Americans instead.

Jung's Tae Kwon Do Academy hosts regular meetings for students who are adopted. Many of my students have chosen to adopt Korean children, because they feel a strong connection to Korea through martial arts knowledge and training. I am thankful to see these kids in loving homes, but I feel sad that the country where I grew up has been so willing to reject their own.

Wise and Humble Americans

I learned from practicing business in the United States that I must plan for the future. While I was building a health club in South Carolina the city government mandated that I use larger-sized gas pipes when smaller ones were sufficient for our needs.

At first I was quite angry that I was required to pay for equipment that I didn't need, but the state official explained to me that even though the area was underdeveloped there were plans in progress to commercially expand it. In the long-run, it would cost more to remove the smaller pipes and put in larger ones. When I found this out, I was happy to comply with the request; I understood the rationale for it.

Although this is only one example of America's philosophy to plan and prepare for the future, I see it traverse everything from building highways to building families to growing up and growing old.

The Power of Eastern and Western Cultures

I have lived 29 years of my life in the East and over 33 years in the West. I have come to recognize significant differences between the two cultures.

I believe the United States is one of the strongest countries in the world, not because of its economic power but because of its value of individual rights and freedoms. For example, in 1997 I visited Beijing, China. While I was there many Chinese people told me that if their economy continues to grow at the rate it has been, it will eventually outgrow the U.S. economy.

However, a Korean-Chinese friend of mine explained, "China might become an economic power and possibly overcome America, but it will take at least 100 years before the Chinese think like Americans, and for their system to value individualism and freedom."

In my opinion, one of the biggest obstacles for Americans is stress — from work, society, and all other social ills. I am still surprised by the number of young people who use drugs, and by the high number of divorces in the United States I find it troubling that so many teens get involved with gangs and crime and end up paying for it for the rest of their lives.

Here in the United States., children can call the police and file a complaint against their parents for alleged misconduct. In Korea, most parents rely on corporal punishment to discipline their children. They do this not because they dislike their kids, but so that the children will learn from their mistakes. The Korean government does not intervene like the government does in the United States.

In America, the government is actively involved in child-rearing. If the state finds a parent's actions unacceptable they will take the child away from them. I used to think this was ridiculous, but now I understand that not all parents possess the ability to make good decisions. For the small number of kids who become victims of abuse or neglect, the government stands on their side.

I learned from living in America that individuality is at the heart of this country and that not even the government can take it away.

After the September 11 attacks, I read a newspaper article that claimed the terrorist attacks were a result of Americans discounting Islam. In Korea, if anyone would have written such an article they would have been considered a public enemy, and they might have faced death threats. The underlying principal of this is that people in the United States are willing to accept the opinions of others in order to maintain and uphold their individual rights.

If someone were to ask me what I have learned during the 30 years I have lived here, I would tell them that happiness is worth far more than money. I am a Tae Kwon Do master who teaches the importance of modesty, love, respect, diligence, and mental strength and I have tried to live according to my philosophy. While the wealth I acquired in this country is small, I plan to dedicate it to helping others attain peace and contentment with themselves.

Chapter 29

Reflections on Life at 60

In February 2002, I turned 60. In the past, not many people have lived beyond this age in Korea. The 60th birthday holds a special meaning for Koreans and calls for a celebration. Three hundred of my students gathered together for this occasion. We drank tea and had homemade wine that one of my students provided. It was a wonderful day and I was happy to celebrate this occasion with them.

I feel blessed to have known people who love and respect me regardless of my flaws; there are many such people in my life. I still can't speak English very well, even after living in this country for 30 years. I am not familiar with computers and I don't know how to use the Internet. I am short and am nothing to look at. I was not the brightest kid in school and didn't do particularly well, and I have a tendency to depend on other people, which I believe results from having been the youngest child in my family.

In 1996, I built an octagon-shaped log cabin on a rocky mountain in Colorado, at 9,500 feet elevation. I named it "Eagles Nest." It is not my vacation home, but it is a sanctuary for anyone who wants to find himself or herself. At least once a year, I drive 25 hours to visit the Eagles Nest and reexamine my life. A young college professor who once stayed there wrote in the log, "I came here thinking I know who I am. I learned I don't, and I leave now to find out."

Today, when I look out from the Eagles Nest, I see scenes from my life come and go. I recall family memories and the faces of those who made my American dream come true. I remember those humble and hard beginnings and feel the spirit of the East in my heart and the dreams of the West before me.

Epilogue

September 1, 2003, marked an important milestone in my life. It marked the 30th anniversary of the opening of my first Tae Kwon Do school in America, as well as the first publication in English of my book *Eastern Spirit, Western Dreams*. I invited my family, my Tae Kwon Do students past and present, and many people who have worked with me over the years to share with me in a celebration of this landmark occasion. Nearly 500 people attended the banquet and ceremonies in Cedar Rapids, Iowa.

The event started with a special candle-lighting ceremony. This ceremony symbolically retraced my journey from South Korea to America, and up to the present day. Participants took the stage throughout the rest of the evening to recount their memories of my life. It was a wonderful evening for me, but I also felt sad, because I thought of those who were no longer living, as well as others who were not able to attend. I felt humble also, compelled to apologize for any mistakes I had made and also to thank those who had helped me find success.

Late in 2003, I was saddened to learn of the death of a former black belt student of mine, the pilot of an Army helicopter shot down in Iraq during Operation Iraqi Freedom. It reminded me of how much the Western dream of freedom means in America; this wonderful young man made the ultimate sacrifice for the cause of freedom. I fervently hope that the whole world may someday share this most important dream of freedom.

The phrase "Eastern Spirit" has been used in this book to represent self-discipline, determination, and respect for others, qualities that form the foundation of character that developed in me as I grew up in Korea. The phrase "Western Dreams" represents my desire to achieve my goal of successfully contributing to society, while living in freedom from poverty, oppression, and social control.

I hope that everyone in the world can experience his or her own "eastern spirit" and "western dreams." The Eastern world needs to ensure individual freedom so that people can live without fear, expressing themselves and building lives based on joy and individual achievement. The Western world needs a reawakening of a spirit of discipline, confidence, and respect for others; modern conveniences must not be allowed to set a tone of laziness or social isolation.

The world, now more than ever, needs to find a deeper respect for life, combining the heart and the spirit with knowledge and understanding. My hope is that we can all find peace, perhaps through our *Western spirit* and our *Eastern dreams*.